MEMORIES LOST AND FOUND

A Search for Family Heritage

ROBERT J. TAYLOR

outskirts
press

Memories Lost and Found
A Search for Family Heritage
All Rights Reserved.
Copyright © 2019 Robert J. Taylor
v4.0

The opinions expressed in this manuscript are solely the opinions of the author and do not represent the opinions or thoughts of the publisher. The author has represented and warranted full ownership and/or legal right to publish all the materials in this book.

This book may not be reproduced, transmitted, or stored in whole or in part by any means, including graphic, electronic, or mechanical without the express written consent of the publisher except in the case of brief quotations embodied in critical articles and reviews.

Outskirts Press, Inc.
http://www.outskirtspress.com

Paperback ISBN: 978-1-9772-0870-5

Cover Photo © 2019 Thomas A. Porter. All rights reserved - used with permission.

Outskirts Press and the "OP" logo are trademarks belonging to Outskirts Press, Inc.

PRINTED IN THE UNITED STATES OF AMERICA

To my mother, and yours

Hildur Florence Back Taylor (1990)

Cover photo: Back homestead cabin, Waskish, Minnesota (Circa 1909)

Contents

1: LOST 1
2: THE SEARCH BEGINS 6
3: A TREE FELL IN THE WOODS 10
4: A WOMAN OF CONSEQUENCE 15
5: A LOG CABIN IN THE FAR NORTH 21
6: FAMILY REUNION 28
7: IMMIGRANT DREAMS 33
8: NO-MAN'S-LAND 39
9: CAT-IN-A-HAT 42
10: COD-SLAB CHRISTMAS 47
11: BARREL MINISTRY 55
12: HOMESTEADER'S HOLIDAY 61
13: LOG-CABIN YULE 67
14: RESILIENT AND DETERMINED 70
15: A WALK THROUGH THE SNOW
    TO A ONE-ROOM SCHOOL 76
16: SPRING'S PROMISE BROKEN 82
17: POOR IN NAME ONLY 89
18: FRUITS OF THE FOREST 92
19: PARTRIDGE IN A BARE TREE 95
20: ONE-SHOT PETE 98
21: ANOTHER MOUTH TO FEED 102
22: THE EYES HAVE IT 106

23: BREAST MILK AND HORSEFLIES	107
24: THE DECISION	112
25: MONTANA MEMORIES	116
26: WIDE-OPEN SPACES	118
27: SODBUSTERS	123
28: HARSH AND BRUTAL LAND	132
29: PAINFUL RECOLLECTIONS	139
30: HEARTACHE AND HEROICS	141
31: NEXT-YEAR COUNTRY	149
32: BROKEN DREAMS	156
33: EMBARRASSED	161
34: PAST AND FUTURE WORLDS	163
35: PASSING ON A LEGACY	166
36: DUPONT ALLEY	171
37: CAR WARS	178
38: FROM WIFE TO WIDOW	185
39: HERE AND NOW AND FAR AWAY	191
40: ROCKY MOUNTAIN HIGH	198
41: MOTHER'S WIT AND WISDOM	201
42: CELEBRATION OF LIFE	205
43: FOUND	210
AFTERWORD	215
ACKNOWLEDGMENTS	219
NOTES	223

1

LOST

"Who are you? Why are you being so nice to me?" she asked, puzzled, as if she should know the answer.

We were in the outdoor courtyard of Jones-Harrison Residence, a stately campus of red brick buildings on the shores of Cedar Lake in Minneapolis. It was late spring and a showy profusion of pink and purple flowers lined our meandering pathway. A blue butterfly flitted among the blossoms. The faint earthy perfume of fresh mulch lingered in the warming air.

My fingers squeezed the handles of her wheelchair, my tongue suddenly caught in my throat. *I should have seen this coming.* The scene froze in place, the butterfly delicately suspended in space forever in my memory.

I took a deep breath. "I'm your son," I whispered.

"What did you say?" she said.

At first I thought she didn't believe me but then realized she couldn't hear. "I'm your son," I said more loudly.

She nodded her head but didn't say another word.

Is this how it ends? I had come to accept my mother's fading memory, her physical decline. I was saddened, but not surprised, to watch her slowly becoming lost to us, the inevitable waning away of a warm and wise woman, the calm and loving stalwart of the Taylor family. It hadn't occurred to me that we—my wife and I, and my brothers and sisters, her whole family—were becoming lost to her.

No, already lost to her.

My wife, Sue, looked stricken. She glanced at me and her face turned to shadow, a sad smile on her lips. She reached out her hand and touched me lightly on the arm.

My mother had been unusually reserved that morning when we went to her room to pick her up. Sue and I had flown in to visit. Mom had been quiet and uncertain until we explained we had come to take her for a walk in the garden. "Oh, I'd like that," she said.

I wheeled her down the hallway as Sue walked by her side. "How are you, Hildur?" Sue asked.

Mom looked up and said, "I'm fine," but offered no elaboration. When we got to the elevator, she asked, "Where are we going?"

Again, I explained, "We're going for a walk in the garden and then we'll have lunch together."

We exited the elevator and pushed through the door to the courtyard, a garden oasis surrounded by the walls of the nursing home. "Oh, it's such a beautiful day," Mom said, looking up at the clear blue sky.

We walked slowly, pausing frequently as Mom reached out to cup a flower between her fingers and draw it to her face. "How lovely," she repeated with each new bloom, "how lovely."

Then, unexpected, her heart-wrenching question, "Who are you?"

At the time, Sue and I lived in Annapolis, Maryland, the restless and wayward members of our immediate families. Everyone else—all our brothers and sisters and their spouses—had tenaciously clung to the Minneapolis area, firmly planted in home ground, steeled to Minnesota's mosquitos and mockingly cold winters. We came to visit as often as we could, picking our seasons.

Had it been only three years since my mother had come to visit us in Annapolis? My sister, Gail, had put her on a non-stop flight into Baltimore Washington International. "Mom's able to get around just fine," Gail said in a telephone call, "but she's getting a little forgetful." We requested a special pass to greet her at the arrival gate.

There is no city more beautiful than our nation's capital in the spring and the city put on a glorious display. It was early April and the cherry trees were in full cotton-candy pink as we strolled around the Tidal Basin on our way to the Jefferson Memorial. We drove Rock Creek Parkway and spotted purple crocuses belatedly pushing up through compacted leaves in shaded corners, reluctantly giving way to yellow daffodils flashing golden in the dappled sun. We drove along the Potomac and stopped to wander in a small park with a painstakingly designed garden planted in a patriotic profusion of red and white tulips.

Early in her visit, as we paused in a copse of flowering fruit trees, Mom said, "This is such a beautiful city. What do you do here?"

I explained that Sue and I were consultants. We traveled a lot, working in developing countries for the United States Agency for International Development (USAID), the World Bank, and others.

"Oh, that's important work," she said.

Fifteen minutes later she asked the same question, "What do you do here?"

I answered again with more elaboration, thinking she hadn't understood.

She nodded her head and said, "That's nice. That's good."

That afternoon she asked again.

In the evening we took her to the Chart House, a fine restaurant in Annapolis overlooking the Severn River and the Naval Academy across the harbor. Over dinner she asked again, "What do you do here?" I answered patiently, remembering Gail's warning, and elaborated on how much fun it was to live in the DC area.

When our volcano-cake dessert arrived, Mom spooned a bit of the molten chocolate oozing from the top. "I've never had this," she said and then glanced around the crowded dining room. "This is fun. Such a nice place and all these important people." At the end of the evening, when the waiter brought our bill, Mom was incredulous. "When you're the guest of the president, you shouldn't have to pay."

Okay. We were in the nation's capital where we do important work and Mom thought our elaborate meal was being hosted by the president of the United States. It was a natural mistake any mother could make.

At the time Sue and I thought it funny but it was a harbinger of Mom's relentless decline due to Alzheimer's. Over the next few years, in our periodic visits to Minneapolis, we noticed her slow progression of memory loss: forgetfulness, struggling for the right word, difficulty making plans, confusion.

For several years after my father died Mom had lived alone in the long-time family home in south Minneapolis. As her forgetfulness increased, my sister Gail arranged for a live-in companion. I wasn't sure if our effort to keep Mom at home was for her benefit or ours. That old house was where all six of us kids had been raised—me and my two older sisters and three younger brothers. It had been the center of family gatherings for decades. It was where we celebrated every Christmas Eve in memory. It was where we came together every October for a collective birthday celebration. Over the years Mom housed a string of nieces and nephews and grandchildren, including our daughter, Jennifer. Sue and I were living in Pakistan at the time, and Jennifer boarded with Mom for a year while she attended her senior year of high school.

Hiring an in-house companion prolonged Mom's move to a nursing home by a year or so, and it gave us all time to come to terms with the inevitable. At first Mom was able to get by in an assisted-living one-room apartment with a small kitchen where she could prepare some of her meals. Safe under the watchful eye of the nursing home staff, she began to rely more and more on meals served in the congregate dining room. Her move to skilled-nursing care came all too quickly.

She seemed happy in the nursing home. "They're nice people," she had said repeatedly. She would often add, with a pouting look on her face, "I eat so much that I'm mournful." She would pause a beat to be sure you were listening. "That's more-than-full," she'd say, a delighted twinkle in her eye.

That twinkle was gone now, just a flicker shared with a flitting butterfly.

Still gripping the wheelchair, I stared at the top of Mother's head, her thinning gray hair yellowing at the fringes. *You don't know who I am. You don't know Sue. I have to ask Gail if you recognize her.* I put my hand on her shoulder and she stiffened ever so slightly. One of her nursing attendants had told us that she seemed wary and fearful, that she didn't always recognize her or other members of the staff.

What must it be like to lose everything? I wondered. It's not like a tornado or flood when overnight you lose all your worldly possessions, or when you lose a loved one to sudden illness or accident. It must be more subtle, the slow eroding of awareness that those things or those people were part of your life. Is that it?

I imagined Mom sitting on the end of a dock watching the mist rise over the lake, a fog drifting toward her, the trees on the far shore indistinct and fading. The thickening fog creeps closer, slowly obliterating everything around her until she can barely see her fingertips at the end of her outstretched arms.

But that scene assumes her awareness. I think it's more like a nagging discomfort with ill-defined anxiety as confusion and disorientation dominate your consciousness and all you know and love fade into oblivion. All that's left is the here and now—the smell of a spring flower or the flutter of a blue butterfly.

Oh, Mom, I thought, *everyone's a stranger. You've lost everybody you love and all you've known.*

2

THE SEARCH BEGINS

Mom was fading more quickly than I realized, and with her, her memories of her family, her history, her life. I had hoped to tell Mother's story, a classic American myth: born to Swedish immigrant, delivered by a midwife, raised in a log cabin in the Minnesota north woods, she walked two miles through the snow to a one-room school.

I wanted to know what shaped her, who or what had made her into whom she was: a gentle and loving soul, funny, inclusive, and non-judgmental. She savored a good cup of coffee as she eased into her mornings, knew the value of doing nothing, was present in the moment, watched the birds and squirrels for at least a little while each day, and looked forward with optimism and courage to whatever her day might bring.

Some of my earliest memories were of my mother talking about growing up in the north woods. It was especially exciting when she got together with her younger brother who pressed her for details about living in a cabin, or when she reminisced with one or more of her four sisters who came to visit from Bemidji.

The stories were often repeated over the years, but I didn't realize their richness and relevance to her life—or my own—until I was well past middle age. And it wasn't until my mother began to experience memory loss that I began to realize how fragile the stories of my heritage were. I decided I needed to document them before they evaporated, lost forever in the firmament. I could stitch together spare fragments, but I wanted to know so much more and I needed my mother to talk to me. Now, any hope I had of drawing her out, her filling in the details, was lost. My other sources—my mother's surviving sisters and her brother who held pieces of the story—were rapidly aging and what they knew would soon be lost as well.

I knew Mom's siblings pretty well. I'd spent time with each of them over the years—individually and collectively. We had caught up on life events when we saw each other—How you feeling? How's the family? Any travel plans? But I had never really interviewed them. I'd never asked, "What's your story?" If I was going to learn what I wanted to know, I would have to be more purposeful. I would have to probe beyond the easy answers and listen with intensity.

I started with a telephone call to my Uncle Glenn, Mom's younger brother.

Uncle Glenn was in his late seventies when I called, still tall and good looking even though the dark wavy hair of his youth had faded to gunmetal gray. But even over the phone I could hear his undiminished vitality and enthusiasm, his zest for life, and it was easy to imagine his ready smile and the twinkling sparkle in his eye.

Glenn Vernon Back (1999)

When I was four or five he lived with us in Minneapolis while he attended the University of Minnesota, after serving as a Marine in the Second World War. Like so many other visiting relatives over time, he slept in the small bedroom behind our kitchen.

He was my favorite uncle, more like an older brother. I followed him around the house like a puppy dog. Every afternoon I'd wait for him to come home from school. I'd sit on the back of the sofa looking out the window, watching for him to walk up the sidewalk from the streetcar stop. When I saw him, I'd climb up three or four steps on the inside stairway just opposite the entryway. When Glenn stepped through the door, I'd launch myself into the air, leaping into his strong hands. While I shrieked in delight he'd say, "Gotcha!" and rub my head with his fist.

Much later, Glenn told me he would put down all his books on the outdoor stoop. He didn't dare walk in the house with anything in his hands. "You had more confidence in me than I did," he chuckled.

"So, Glenn," I said into the telephone, "I'm trying to pull together some stories about my mother, and your folks, Peter and Lena. You know, the homestead cabin and such."

"Well," Glenn began, "I was born after they moved to Bemidji so I never lived in the cabin. That was your mom and my sisters. I did go to school up at Waskish for a couple of years, but that was later, when my folks were managing the Sunset Lodge for the road crew. So I know the territory, but by then they had long abandoned the homestead."

He paused before continuing. "You know, by golly, I've got a cassette tape of your mother. A few years ago I interviewed her about life up at the cabin."

"Oh! I'd really like to get that. I don't have any recordings of Mom's voice."

"I've got it around here somewhere," Glenn said. "I'll look for it."

"Please do. But for now, to get me started, tell me what you know."

"Well, there's a lot to tell. Both my mom and dad immigrated in 1902. They were from Sweden but they didn't meet until after they arrived here, in Holmes City, near Alexandria. That's where they got married."

Glenn paused. In the quiet, I could almost hear his wheels turning before he went on, "Dad was a woodsman, you know."

"He's the one member of your family I never met," I said. Peter Back (pronounced Bach, like Johann Sebastian), died in April, 1940, eight months before I was born. "Maybe that's why I have this romantic image of him," I continued. "It's like a movie running in my head: a sturdy and good-natured lumberjack."

"He was that, all right, but there's so much more to the story" Glenn continued in a rush of words. "He was almost thirty years old when he arrived here. He was with his brother. They walked across the border from Canada. His last name was Hjelm but he changed it to Back."

"Whoa!" I interjected. "Slow down. I'm trying to take notes."

"Sorry," he said. "I'm excited you're doing this and, oh, there's so much to tell…"

3

A TREE FELL IN THE WOODS

Peter Back extended his left arm, his mittened hand gripping the helve of his axe, its two-bladed head pointing toward an eight-foot open space between two young aspen trees. "Yeah, right there," he said in Swedish. The sound of his voice was instantly absorbed into the silent void of the surrounding forest.

Peter lowered the axe to his side and stood for a moment listening to the quiet. Usually there was some sound in the woods: the murmur of wind, branch brushing against branch, or the staccato drumming of a pileated woodpecker. Or there were sounds of his own making: the squeak of his boots treading through the dry snow, the thunk of his axe biting into wood. Sometimes there was the sound of his voice, talking to himself, giving himself instructions, complimenting a task well done or mildly cursing at a task gone wrong. Often, the brassy richness of his enthusiastic baritone singing a stanza from a favorite Swedish melody rang through the forest.

But now, at this moment, on this splendid December day in the year 1913, there was absolute silence. The sky was a cerulean blue, not a cloud evident through the overhanging branches. The air was crisp and cold with no hint of a breeze. The faint scent of pine and woodchips hung in the still air. The sun filtered low through the trees, frugally dappling light on the fresh, unbroken snow; shadows of blue and black hid in the deep hollows beneath low-hanging spruce boughs where even summer's sun was a stranger. Peter held his breath to quiet his own breathing, aware of the blood flowing in his head, the thump of his heartbeat. *If there's a God*, Peter thought, *He's here now.*

"Enough," Peter whispered, the plume of his breath frosting his dark mustache. He had already chopped a wedge on the opposite side of the tree, on the side facing the space between the two aspens. He lifted the axe, gripping it firmly in both hands. His feet spread, he rotated his shoulders slightly to his right. He brought the axe back about waist high, then swiftly forward, rotating his body into the stroke and driving the blade into the trunk about two feet above the snow. A loud "thwack" broke the silence, a chip of wood as big as Peter's hand flew through the air landing among others, a pattern of gray-red bark and yellow chips covering the snow in a six-foot circle around the base of the tamarack, a thirty-five foot conifer rising upward, straight and true, into the thin forest canopy.

He took another stroke, then another.

He paused, took a step back, and extended his arm once again, but this time he placed the axe head against the trunk of the tree and leaned into it. "There you go," he said, giving the tree encouragement to do the inevitable. Which it did, hesitant at first, a splintering crack, a nod toward the intended target. Then, with growing certainty, the trunk twisted from its stump and lost its grip on the earth. Its fall accelerated as it dragged its reluctant branches from the sky. Boughs snapped and cracked. There was a heavy thud and a ground shudder that Peter could feel through his boots. With a whoosh of air a cloud of snow rose on the scent of fresh cut wood, sending crystals spinning and floating and sparkling into the filtered sunlight.

And then, again, silence.

Those silent woods were part of what was once a vast forest of towering red pine (called Norway pine by Minnesotans and designated the state tree), mixed with gigantic white and jack pine that stretched two thousand miles across America's far north, following the shores of the Great Lakes from the Atlantic Ocean to the Minnesota/Dakota border, and northward into Canada's mid-section.[1] The virgin forest had carpeted gently rolling terrain, a stretch of ground raised ever-so-slightly on the northern steppes of the Laurentian Plateau, the Canadian Shield, an ancient U-shaped formation of mountains and up-thrust rock that extends from northern Minnesota, east along Canada's southern border, then north to the Arctic Circle.[2] The Plateau is now a boggy and wet expanse of lightly-populated land, pockmarked with thousands of lakes scooped out during the Pleistocene epoch. The lingering shadow of those ancient mountains forms the transcontinental divide, similar to the continental divide in the western Rocky Mountains. However, here on the northern slope of the Laurentian Chain where Peter leaned on his axe contemplating the quiet, water flows to the Red River and northward to Hudson Bay. A few miles to the south, on the other side of a slight rise, water works its way to the Gulf of Mexico.

Most of the big timber in northern Minnesota was logged well before Peter arrived. During the lumber boom of 1880 and 1890 the prime timber was decimated by big lumber companies, logged to meet the needs of a growing America. On the lands near where Peter stood, logs as thick as a man is tall were cut and stacked fifteen feet high on sleds pulled by teams of draft horses over frozen roads to Kelliher, then by train to Bemidji where they were rolled onto the ice of the upper Mississippi. With the spring thaw, the huge logs were floated two hundred miles south to Minneapolis where they jammed the river above the sawmills at Saint Anthony Falls. Logs were so thick and tight you could—with spiked boots, a sure step and a timberman's pike—walk from the banks of Minneapolis across five hundred undulating yards of river to the shores of Saint Anthony Village.[3]

It wasn't until the big timber companies were satiated that the land was opened up for homesteading. In 1913, when Peter felled his tamarack, all that remained of the once vast forest in his part of Minnesota was second-growth trees—aspen, tamarack, spruce, cedar, and fir—poking up from a thicket of underbrush of willow, juniper, and poison ivy.

Today, more than a hundred years after Peter's time, you can still find a few large stands of mammoth pines along the Minnesota/Canadian border—most notably in the Superior National Forest, part of the Boundary Waters Canoe Area. But in Peter's part of Minnesota, on the eastern shores of Upper Red Lake, all that remains are a few scattered clumps of tall "seeder" trees, preserved in the vain hope they would repopulate the decimated forest.

Peter stood for a moment watching the cloud of snow hanging in the air. A wavering rainbow appeared, then faded as the crystals settled back onto the white carpet. He wiped his brow with the back of his mitten, then dabbed a drop of moisture from the end of his nose. The faint smell of wool and leather tickled his nostrils. He took off his black fur hat and placed it on top of the fresh cut stump. The steam from his matted hair swirled in a halo around his head. His brother's wife, Sigrid Olson, had she been there, might have said she saw his aura—pink and purple—the sign of a man who enjoys life, a spiritual man at peace with himself.

Peter removed his mittens, laying them atop his fur hat. Mist rose from his thick-fingered hands. He preferred to work bare-handed but the day had started out brutally cold. That morning he had stepped out of the cabin and spit at a tree stump he used to split stove-wood. His spittle had clinked off the stump like lead shot. "Colder than a county commissioner's heart," he muttered, as he donned his hat and mittens. By mid-morning it was still cold, the sun's heat thin and reluctant, but he was comfortably warm, in fact a bit too warm from working in his long underwear, thick wool pants, wool shirt and canvas coat.

He stepped toward the fallen tree, his boots sinking into the powdery snow to mid-calf. This tamarack, like all larches, was a botanical oxymoron, a deciduous-pine that sheds its needles each winter. Its branches were bare except for a smattering of small ovoid cones clinging stubbornly. With quick, sure strokes of his axe, Peter began to strip the branches from the trunk. Starting at the bottom he worked his way up one side of the trunk, tossing severed boughs aside as he moved up to the crown. Then back to the base and up the other side. He gave the fallen tree a heavy push with his boot, rolling it enough to clear the few remaining branches that clung underneath.

He gathered up the branches and stacked them against the trunk of an aspen where they would rest through spring. When dry, they would make good stove kindling, the resinous sap quick to light and the cones adding a pleasing pop to the fire.

Peter leaned his axe against the tree stump. Picking up a four-foot crosscut bow saw, a Swede's saw, and returning to the fallen tree, he sawed off its ragged base with long firm strokes, the saw cutting on both the push and draw. His first cut squared up the butt end, a yellow disk sixteen inches in diameter. He then used the saw to mark off and cut the log into two ten foot sections. The remaining top section, too thin for sale, he cut into four foot lengths, laying each smaller log on the pile of branches.

Peter stepped away from his work. "One down, four more to go," he said. He looked up from the resting logs, noting a dozen tamarack within his view. He knew there were several hundred more on his land, hidden from his sight but the location of nearly every one etched in his memory.

Peter ended the day, the sun low in the trees, with ten ten-foot logs lying in the woods, each bedded down in a blanket of snow. Tomorrow he would bring Good-Old-Jim, his black and white ox, to help muscle the logs onto a sled. The day after, he'd hitch up the horses and haul the load into Kelliher to be sold to the lumber yard where they would be cut into railroad ties or used to construct log buildings.

As the light began to lengthen, turning the white snow to gold, he leaned on his axe admiring his day's work. But a disquieting thought, intrusive and unwelcome, shadowed his mind, *Lena's right, it's not enough.*

4

A WOMAN OF CONSEQUENCE

My first memory of Grandma Lena Back was when I was three, when I fell in the lake. Even after more than seventy years, I still vividly remember lying on the sandy bottom, looking up through the water to the surface, the images above in greens and whites, fragmented and unfocused. I don't remember having any sense of fear or panic; rather a detached calm, a quietness.

I was attending a family reunion at Hall's Moose Lake Resort, a conclave of small cabins—owned by my mother's sister, Elvera, and her husband Delbert Hall—situated on a remote lake about an hour's drive outside Bemidji, Minnesota. The last mile into the resort was along a narrow dirt road, two ruts winding through bog and woods, an unending stretch of muddy potholes and the scratch of pine boughs brushing against the side of the car. As a distraction from the road's worrisome condition, my Uncle Del had nailed humorous signs to trees here and there along the margin. One read "Winding Road," followed several curves later with "Unwinding Road." The ominous "Sink Hole Ahead" brought near panic to first-time visitors until they went around the next curve where an old white porcelain kitchen sink was propped up against a tree, a red arrow pointing to the drain. The last sign on the road instructed "Honk Your Horn" and signaled your approach to the resort.

The resort was neat and simple. Eight uninsulated cabins were numbered in order as they stretched along the shoreline, each with a small wood-burning stove, a linoleum-topped dining table, a few mismatched chairs, and a couple of rope-cot beds. There was also an ice-box that Uncle Del stocked each day with ice chipped from large blocks sawed from the lake in deep winter and packed with sawdust in a two-story icehouse at the edge of the forest. The icehouse was near a small barn where Del milked a cow, Daisy Mae. The cow helped Del trim the grass around the cabins. What Daisy May didn't eat, Del mowed with a long-bladed scythe. There was no electricity—except for a couple of hours each evening when Del cranked an old John Deere generator into life. Its main task was to pump lake water into a tank atop the central shower house, but it also produced just enough energy to light one bulb in each of the cabins through the twilight hours. The Rural Electrical Association didn't bring electricity to that northern backcountry until 1948, when I was seven years old.

The sink in each cottage drained into a bucket that Del emptied when he brought in the day's ration of ice for the icebox. There was an iron-stained white-enamel pail to carry water from the centrally located hand-pump, next to the horseshoe pits over which a colony of purple martins sored and swooped to keep the mosquito hoards at bay. The outhouses were outback by the wood pile. Each cabin had three luxuries: a screened porch looking out toward the lake, a private dock, and a fishing boat with oars. You could rent a pull-crank outboard motor and buy minnows for fishing.

I had been standing on one of those docks, the long one in front of Number-One Cabin, with a crowd of older cousins and a few adults full of animated chatter, gesturing and pointing at a big man named Tiny holding a large fish dangling from a stringer. Then a bumping hip and I was in the water, on the bottom, flat on my back, looking up at the surface.

I raised my arm and stretched my hand toward the light. A face took shape above the surface and a hand reached down. The fingers firmly griped my wrist. With one strong pull I was up through the water and back on the dock. My grandmother's face was close to mine, a large bun of red hair mounded on her head, her hand still wrapped around my wrist. It is one of my first memories of any kind—her eyes looking me over and then, with a matter-of-fact smile and a pat on my wet head, she was back with the others, congratulating Tiny on his big catch.

A year or two later, when I was five or six, I was kneeling on a chair, my elbows on the dining room table at our home in Minneapolis. Grandma Back sat sipping coffee, a cube of sugar between her teeth and lip, round-rimmed glasses perched on her nose. She had a piece of thin cardboard and scissors laid out in front of her. My mother was in the kitchen baking caramel rolls. The heady smell of cinnamon and yeast filled the house.

"What would you like me to make?" Grandma asked. She spoke grammatically perfect English but with a noticeable Swedish accent.

She knew I liked to play with crayons and cut out paper shapes to make crude houses and cars that I used with figures I modeled out of clay.

Before I could respond she said, "How about an airplane?"

"Yes, please," I said, as I watched her cut a round flower-like piece with square petals around the circumference. "What's that," I asked, as she placed the finished piece on the table.

"You'll see," she said. "Be patient."

It was the mid-1940s, just after the War. In those years, Grandma Back was a regular presence in my young life. Two or three times a year she came to Minneapolis. Sometimes she'd stay with my Aunt Claire, but frequently she stayed with us, claiming the small bedroom behind our kitchen. She didn't give us kids much attention, usually devoting her time to knitting, or reading, or conversations with my mother. She smiled at us kids, but I never sat in her lap and I never heard her laugh. So, being with her alone at the table as she snipped and cut was a rare event. Even if she didn't say much, she had my full attention.

"What's that?" I asked, as she placed a long and narrow piece of cardboard among the growing array of cutouts.

"It's a wing," she said, as she cut another piece of the same shape.

For what must have been an hour I watched in rapt attention as she industriously snipped away at paper and cardboard, fitting pieces together with bobby pins plucked from her hair, toothpicks and a paste made from flour and water.

While Grandma worked, my mother brought out a plate of fried dough, round patties of leftover sweet-roll dough she fried in butter. They had been brushed with butter and sprinkled with powdered sugar and cinnamon. She also set out a plate with sections of tangerine arrayed like flower petals around a mound of powdered sugar. "Here you go," she said as she picked a stray strand of pith from one of the fruit sections..

While I enjoyed a bite of fried dough, Grandma continued her work. Between bites I took a section of tangerine, dipped it in the powdered sugar, and popped it in my mouth.

When Grandma finished, I was in awe with the results: a small biplane with an open cockpit, a round engine cowling (the square-petaled flower), and a popsicle-stick propeller—all standing on a paperclip tail-skid and two button wheels.

"Be careful," she said as she handed it to me and reached for a piece of fried dough. "It's not very sturdy."

"Thank you," I said, as I set it down in the center of the dining room buffet.

I didn't dare play with it. But every day I would spend a moment admiring that airplane. I think I was as awed by my grandma's attention as I was by the creativity of her handiwork. The biplane stayed on the buffet for weeks until it was displaced by platters and bowls piled with food for some family gathering. I never saw the airplane again. And I never again had that much personal time with my grandmother.

In the summers that followed, our family would all jam into the car—Dad, Mom, and one of us kids in front, with three or four in the back—and we'd drive from Minneapolis to Bemidji. I loved the trip, especially if we took old Highway 169 along the western shore of Lake Mille Lacs where Native Americans sold toy birch-bark canoes and painted lake scenes rendered on bias-cut ovals of pine or birch. When we got to Brainerd we kids would try to be the first to spot the pink façade of Van's Café where we'd stop for lunch. On the last leg up to Bemidji we'd play road games—alphabet or, to my father's consternation, sing one-hundred-bottles-of-beer-on-the-wall. Our last stop before Grandma's house was on the shores of Lake Bemidji where Mom bought us ice cream cones and we walked among the legs of the giant concrete statues of Paul Bunyan and Babe, his blue ox.

Grandma Back lived on the second floor of a home she owned across the street from the Bemidji High School. Rent from the lower unit and a couple of bedrooms upstairs were a major source of her income. Her upstairs apartment was spare, with a closet cubbyhole for her sewing and craft projects and paint-by-number pictures mounted on the walls. A clear plastic slipcover protected the couch and white doilies decorated every chair. An oval rag-stock rug adorned the living room floor.

If the downstairs apartment was vacant we might stay the night, but usually we just stopped by to pick her up. No hugs or kisses, we nodded hello and unceremoniously squeezed Grandma and her small bag into the car—my mother said, "There's always room for one more"—and drove out to Hall's Resort where we rented a cabin for a week. Sometime during that week, while Dad went fishing with Uncle Del or helped him with some building project he had going, Grandma Back would lead her daughters on a berry-picking excursion, and I'd tag along, too small to be left on my own. Depending on the season, we'd forage for wild raspberries, or those sweet little wild strawberries that hid in the tall grass along the side of the road, or go to the blueberry bog where I'd stain my fingers and lips while the ladies filled buckets. I don't think we had a summer meal where we didn't have berry pie, sometimes topped off with home-churned ice cream.

Aunt Elvera would combine sugar and vanilla with the thick cream that rose to the top of Daisy Mae's fresh milk. The mixture went into a metal canister with a paddle insert that attached to a crank. The whole paraphernalia fit inside a wooden tub that had been gnawed on by some wild beast. "A porcupine chewed on it for the salt," declared Uncle Del. Each of us kids was allowed ten cranks while Uncle Del carefully sprinkled rock salt on the shaved ice surrounding the slowly turning canister. It was declared ice cream when Del was the only one with the strength to make the last few turns.

I remember Grandma Back, business like, serving me a piece of blueberry pie, topped with homemade ice cream she swept off a spoon with her finger.

Grandma Back with Bobby and Tommy (1943)

With all those relatives around, I often overheard comments about life at the old homestead, a cabin in the woods. I had visited the area when I was a child, but my memories were faint. Each summer when we were up north, Mom would drive Grandma up to Waskish, about sixty-five miles northeast of Bemidji, a crossroads on the shores of Upper Red Lake and near the long gone Back family cabin. My only memory of the place was when I was two or three, walking across a low wooden foot bridge, clinging to my mother's hand, petrified of falling through the gaps between the planking into the water flowing below.

When I was older, I had daydreams about that cabin in the woods and over the years, as I heard story after story, I put together a clearer picture of what it must have been like.

5

A LOG CABIN IN THE FAR NORTH

Lena Back looked out the cabin's small window at the night's darkness, the faint image of her face reflected in the glass. Vera, nearly ten, stood by the door churning butter, slowly turning a crank that rotated the paddles inside a large glass jar, agitating the cream within. The three younger girls were at the dining table behind her, murmuring, intent on their play. Hildur, three years old, her brown eyes dancing, stood on a chair watching her older sisters page through a Montgomery Ward's catalog. In the shallow light of an oil lamp the girls were cutting out pictures of flowery hats, frilly dresses and other wonders of the outside world.

"Oh, pretty shoes," said Anna, who was four. "Look at the buttons!"

Clara, who had just celebrated her seventh birthday, dutifully cut out the illustration to which Anna had pointed and placed it on a growing pile of clippings. In the days ahead the girls would spend countless hours sorting through the pieces of paper, selecting their favorites, changing their minds, dreaming of possibilities.

Lena smiled. She had already done the catalog shopping for the season, using much of the cash Peter had earned working the harvest out in North Dakota. She'd ordered a bolt of cloth, a pair of heavy wool pants for Peter, new shoes for each of the girls, and a three-legged cast iron pot, a Dutch oven, for herself. On his last trip into Kelliher, Peter had picked up the parcels from the post office. Even so, there was no harm in letting the girls have this small indulgence. After all, Christmas was less than a week away and each girl would get a gift of some kind on the holiday. There wouldn't be any toys or games, the girls made their own entertainment, but in addition to shoes each girl would get something practical: a hand-sewn dress, mittens, wool socks, or a new wool cap. And they would be pleased and content and the catalog clippings would be forgotten, at least for a while.

The table where the children huddled stood on the cabin's wooden floor, the floorboards worn smooth from the scuff of shoes and frequent scrubbing. Here and there a hard knot, impervious to wear, held defiant, an uneven hump ready to snag a string from Lena's mop or stub the toe of a barefoot child.

A cast iron pot-bellied stove stood in the middle of the floor, the main source of heat in the cabin, augmented by a cast iron cooking stove that sat at the edge of the kitchen lean-to that had been added to the cabin after Lena pointed out to Peter that he had not provided adequate kitchen space when he'd built the place. Fires were stoked and the stovepipes, which rose through the ceiling and warmed the children's sleeping loft above, glowed a soft red. The cabin's log walls were heavily chinked with horsehair and clay and were efficient in keeping in the heat. For a cold winter's evening, the cabin was quite comfortable.

Lena expected Peter at any moment. He had risen well before daylight to take a load of timber into Kelliher; ten tamarack logs roped to a flatbed sled and drawn by two horses. Kelliher was little more than a general store, a lumber yard, a few houses and a railroad station. The trip was thirteen miles each way. The road to town was easier to navigate this time of year. Spring through fall it was either deep ruts of hardened clay or a quagmire of mud. Now into December, the trail was frozen solid as a stone and covered with ice and drifted snow, what Peter called "full-sledding" conditions. It was a long and chilly ride into town and back, but an easy pull for a good team of horses. Lena knew the trip would take all day but the few dollars her husband received for the timber would be most welcome.

As she continued to look out the window, Lena absently licked the tips of two floured fingers and pushed back a lock of red hair from her forehead, tucking it into the large bun twisted and stacked on top of her head. It was dark outside and had been since four-thirty that afternoon, more than an hour ago. The evening was cold and windless and a fine powdering of snow was falling. Looking past her reflection Lena could see small flakes dancing in the pale light from the window, each flake taking its own sweet time before coming to rest, adding a minute crystal to the thin layer of snow already covering the yard. Beyond the window's glow there was blackness so impenetrable on a cloudy and moonless night like tonight one could get lost walking to the outhouse. She was not frightened by the dark. She could have spent the whole evening just watching those snowflakes fall against that black backdrop. She found comfort in the night's quiet and calm.

It's my birthday today, she thought, although she did not expect anybody to acknowledge the fact. *I'm thirty-four years old already and it's over ten years since I left Sweden.* Staring out at that inky blackness she could see herself in her childhood, back in the home-country. She let her mind draw pictures, chalk tracings on a school slate-board.

Härjedalen province sprawls across Sweden's midsection like a wide belt, dividing the country's more urban southern districts from the vast Noorland, or North Land, with its heavily forested low mountains and deep blue lakes stretching north for hundreds of miles to beyond the Arctic Circle. Winters in the North Land are long and severe, with heavy snows and short days. In this beautiful and harsh landscape, on her parent's small farm near the village of Lindsell, Carolina was born to Olof and Katrina Frisk, delivered by a midwife on December 22, 1879.

Lena could only vaguely remember her father, Olof; she was only six when he died in an accident. She knew he had struggled to eke out a living on the family farm. Like most land holdings in the area, the Frisk farm was a few stony acres with a small cabin and a couple of low out-buildings made of rough-cut timbers. Throughout the country, generations of first sons struggled to make a living on farms too small to support a family while their younger brothers worked hard-labor on other people's land. Years of draught had made matters worse. Only a few farms in the North Land, those in the lowlands and river valleys, were larger or better for growing crops.

Olof and Katrina Frisk (Circa 1874)

Olof's major crop had been hay, which he used to feed a few head of dairy cattle. To make ends meet, he and Lena's mother, Katrina, sold milk, cream and butter and did odd jobs. Katrina served as a midwife and Olof hired out to other farmers and timbermen. They raised chickens for eggs and meat and Lena could remember one time when a deer hung from a tree in the yard. Olof also hunted rabbits and caught fish in the nearby lakes. Katrina bought flour and other staples in town but much of the family's food came from her large garden. Lena remembered helping her mother dig up stones from that patch of earth, building rows of lopsided cairns along its borders.

When Olof died, Katrina was left to raise five children—Lena and her three older sisters and one younger brother. Unable to feed the family on her own, Katrina sent the girls to surrounding farms to do housework and farm chores. Lena remembered being sent to a neighbor's farm to herd livestock. For days at a time she stayed at the neighbor's home, slept and ate her meals there, and did her assigned tasks. After several days she could come home for a day or two, then return to work for another several days.

Each morning, Lena remembered, as she was heading out to the pasture to tend the sheep, the woman of the house gave her a piece of bread generously spread with butter. At lunchtime Lena sat down to eat. She cautiously sniffed the bread, and gagged. Again, the butter was rancid! But Lena was hungry and had nothing else to eat. Stoically, not for the first time, she brushed off as much of the butter as she could and forced down the bread. "Oh, how much easier it would be," she had thought, "to just eat the bread dry." Lena could still remember that taste.

On another afternoon, after a stint of several days staying at the neighbor's, Lena began the long walk home to her mother's. On the way she sat down on a low tree stump to rest for a moment. As she sat, she absently ran her fingers through her long hair; it felt like it had sand in it! Puzzled, she showed her hair to her mother when she got home. Lena could still remember her mother's voice, horrified and angry, as she cried, "Lice! You've got lice and nits everywhere! That woman! She can't keep a clean house and here you are with lice in your hair!"

Katrina took Lena out into the yard, well away from the house, and began to run a fine-toothed comb through her hair. After a few minutes she stopped in disgust. "There are too many. Your hair's a mess." Without another word, Katrina picked up a pair of scissors and cut off all of Lena's hair down to within a half-inch of her scalp. She made Lena strip off her clothes and gave her a bath with harsh soap. Later, Katrina washed all of Lena's clothes in boiling water. Her hair clippings were burned in an outside fire.

Without a husband, Katrina struggled alone for a couple of years until a man, Olof Amundson, started visiting the farm. He helped Katrina with repairs, harvested the hay crop, and tended the cattle. After several months he moved into the farmhouse with Katrina, Lena and the other children. A year or so later Katrina gave birth to a boy, John, and in another year or so, another boy, Ole. For her entire life, Lena was never able to get over the embarrassment of her mother living with "that man" to whom she was not married.

In 1898, at the age of sixteen, Lena's younger brother, Peter Frisk, decided to immigrate to America. While younger than most, Peter was following thousands of his countrymen who had already fled Sweden's poverty and required military service. Over a period of seventy years, from 1860 to 1930, over a million Swedish citizens, a quarter of the population, left the country in hope of a better life in America. Lena thought that if her brother hadn't gone to America, the whole family might still be in Sweden. But after a few years, Peter sent money back home and encouraged his mother to sell the farm and join him in America. In 1902, Lena left Sweden with her mother, two of her sisters, Anna and Katrina, and their families. Her mother's paramour, Olof Amundson, and Lena's two half-brothers, Ole and John, also joined them. Only Ericka, Lena's oldest sister, stayed in Sweden.

Lena did not have fond memories of the trip to America. It was long and at times very uncomfortable. From the harbor town of Göteborg, on Sweden's southwest coast, she and her family traveled by boat to London, England. She still got shivers thinking about the tortuous train ride from London to Liverpool when they were crammed together like cattle in a boxcar. From Liverpool they traveled by steamship to New York and arrived at Ellis Island.

Upon entering the country, in the tradition of many Swedish immigrants, they assumed the family name Olson, son of Olof, based on their father's name. Lena thought Olson was a suitable choice since Olof was both her father's name and also the name of her step-father. From New York, Lena Frisk Olson traveled with her family by train to Alexandria, Minnesota, and the nearby town of Holmes City where some of her relatives had already settled.

Lena stared out the cabin window into the blackness. *We're all here now,* she thought. *Mother's right next door; my sisters and brother are all within a few miles. Even that man, Olof Amundson—at least Mother's not living with him.*

A glimmer of light in the outside blackness broke her reverie. She was sure it was the yellow glow from the oil lamp Peter had taken with him. A moment later she heard the squeak of the sled's runners on the snow and the faint sound of her husband's voice, singing. Before Lena could say anything, her second oldest daughter, Clara, looked up and said to her sisters, "Shush! I hear Daddy coming."

As her husband entered the yard, Lena could hear his rich baritone voice, singing to the horses, singing to the heavens, singing to the world, "You old, you free, you northern mountain. You quiet, you happy and beautiful country." It was a line from a folk tune, and the Swedish national anthem, and one of Peter's favorite songs.

Vera set aside the butter churn and quickly gathered up the catalog, scissors, and paper clippings and set them on a low bench against the wall. With practiced efficiency, she and Clara spread a cotton tablecloth over the table's rough wooden surface and began to set out plates and flatware for dinner.

It would take several minutes for Peter to unhitch the sled and settle the horses in the barn. Lena turned away from the window to attend a pot of potatoes boiling on the stove. Into another pot, filled partway with boiling water, she emptied green beans from a two-quart glass jar—one of the many jars of vegetables she had canned last fall and stored in the root cellar. She had baked bread earlier in the day and now a loaf of limpa, a rye bread with a touch of molasses and anise, was tucked in the warming cabinet above the stove.[4] A venison roast was in the oven where it had been cooking in its own gravy for hours, its aroma blending with the smell of the kerosene lamp and wet wool mittens, remnants of an afternoon snowball fight now drying on a line above the pot-bellied stove. Clara placed butter and milk on the table. All was set for dinner.

The girls chirped like chickadees, eager to see their father and excited to know what he might have brought from town. They could all hear him singing, fading in and out as he tended the horses. "You reign in our memory from the days gone by. We'll put on our cap and let your name go all over the world."

At last they heard him stomp his feet outside the door, knocking the snow from his boots.

6
FAMILY REUNION

After talking with my Uncle Glenn, I spent months documenting what I knew and what I imagined about my grandparents and the Back family folk tales. I compiled a timeline of significant events riddled with gaps. I had more questions than answers, but my homework gave me a framework for interviewing my relatives. They might be able to fill in the details. Given their geographic scattering, however, setting up interviews seemed like a daunting task.

Then, an unexpected opportunity.

"We're going to have a family reunion this summer," my sister Gail said on the phone. "We'll meet up at the resort right after Labor Day. I hope you and Sue can come."

"Perfect. We'll be there for sure. I'll make reservations right away."

"Hot damn," I told Sue. "I can catch them all at once."

"What are you talking about?" she said.

"A family reunion, at Moose Lake in September; all my relatives will be there."

"I'll call Jennifer and David," she said. "They'll want to come."

With my mother's memory lost and Glenn's recording still not found, I needed to interview and record those sources that remained: my mother's two living sisters, Claire Porter and Ann Stennes, both with a firm grip on their nineties, and again, Glenn, who was making a run on eighty. Getting them all together at one time, feeding off each other's recollections—seemed like my big chance.

Hall's Moose Lake Resort, the site of so many family vacations when I was a child, had been sold in 1966 when my Aunt Elvera's husband, Delbert, died. That was a bad year for losing uncles. In addition to Del, Aunt Ann's husband, Oscar Stennes, passed away, as did Aunt Claire's husband, Roy Porter.

At the time, we all assumed that the resort was now just a fond memory. But in 1973, a couple of my Stennes cousins, in partnership with a good friend, bought the resort back. They put a lot of sweat and money into the place—modernizing the cabins, adding a club house, and manicuring the grounds. The outhouses were gone and the central shower house abandoned, but the rutted road through the woods didn't improve much, and it didn't get any shorter. They did remove most of the anxiety-producing signs along its winding route.

We gathered for the reunion in September, 1999. Everyone was there—uncles, aunts, cousins, nephews, nieces, and a few shirttail relatives I didn't recognize—everyone but my mother who was by then too incapacitated to travel. A big surprise and an exciting bonus was my distant cousin, Lynn Lanus, who brought a spiral-bound book she had just compiled, *The Hjelm Journey*, where she documented the Hjelm family lineage going back eight generations to 1660, with entrancing stories and vignettes sprinkled throughout.[5] It provided a rich history of Grandpa Peter (Hjelm) Back, and his ancestors, his siblings, and all their progeny.

I talked to Claire and Ann and Glenn, and told them what I was trying to do. They all were excited by the project and were eager to tell what they knew. At the resort, we spent a long evening gathered around the fireplace in one of the new cabins. I had a recorder going and the conversation ranged widely: growing up poor in the north woods, living in a small cabin, walking to a one-room school, and moving to Montana. We went on for a couple of hours and I was thrilled with what I was learning. They mostly agreed on the events but differed a bit in their perspectives. Claire was best on names and details, Ann on the story line, and Glenn on the personalities and emotional content. Together, they added depth and richness to the history.

Still, the conversations raised as many questions as they answered.

I wanted to know so much more. Unfortunately, the pressing schedule of all the reunion events kept me from probing further—a blueberry pie contest, for example (which I won), and a walleye fish-fry—but I did get eager commitments from everyone to talk again in the months ahead.

I got a little more time with my Uncle Glenn when he joined several of us on a day trip up to Kelliher, where we stopped by the North Beltrami Heritage Center[6] and on to Waskish where we visited the old family homestead.

"The path back to the cabin was right about here, I think," Glenn offered, pointing across a deep drainage ditch paralleling the road toward a slight break in the trees overgrown with thistles and brush. "You should be able to find the foundation to the cabin, maybe fifty, a hundred feet back or so. If you don't mind, I'll wait here. Good luck."

"Thanks," I said, as I joined a couple of my cousins bushwhacking through the undergrowth. We were immediately swarmed by mosquitos the size of locusts. "These buggers will drain your body dry," I quipped, but nobody laughed. We stomped around for a few minutes but with all the bugs everyone quickly lost their taste for exploration. We didn't find the foundation or other signs that the plot had ever been settled. My biggest impression of the place, other than the mosquitos, was that it was still a sorry plot of ground. The long-gone big timber had not grown back. The few big trees that stood on widely scattered hillocks had been left standing by loggers a century earlier with the assumption they would reseed the clear-cut forest. They hadn't. The land was much as it had been when Peter Back filed his claim—mostly tamarack, aspen, and birch, with a few pine struggling for purchase in the boggy soil.

When we emerged from the thicket, Glenn said, "You know, it was hard to make a living on this old place. It was really nothing but scrub land. Still is. The big timber was on the hillocks, the low ridgeline where you see those few seeder trees. Most of this land was never worth a damn." He turned his attention to one of my Stennes cousins who was driving. "Do we have time to visit Scenic State Park? It's not very far from here."

Scenic State Park is a surveyor's mistake—3,300 acres of virgin timber never allocated to any of the logging companies that devastated so much of the surrounding forest, including Peter's land. It was set aside as a preserve in 1921.[7] As we exited the car, I was stunned by the towering canopy of trees that surrounded us. As we followed the path through the forest we stopped by a Norway red pine, a hundred feet tall, with a trunk so large it took the arm-span of two of us, plus Uncle Glenn's shoulder girth, to reach around its circumference.

Tree hugging in Scenic State Park

The undergrowth among the big trees was spare, stunted by a niggardly allotment of filtered sunlight and smothered by centuries of falling pine needles. The diary of a long ago forest fire was etched in the trunks of some of the trees—hollow conical scars where downwind eddies of super-heated gas burned away the scaly plates of their red bark.

I was awestruck. "I didn't know this was here," I said. "It's like standing among the giant redwoods in Muir Woods."

Glenn looked up into the unbroken canopy and swept his arm in a wide arch. "This is what your grandfather's land looked like before it was logged," he said. He shook his head sadly. "I think they thought it would all grow back."

That evening, after Glenn had won eight straight games of pool, beating all comers, I asked him, "So, Glenn, don't you ever let somebody else win?"

"Absolutely not," he said. "It's the way I played basketball, it's the way I play cards—I play to win. It's a matter of integrity and respect."

I should have asked him where he learned to play pool so well. There was a story there, I'm sure.

Glenn paused and took a sip of beer. "By the way," he continued, "I've looked through all the boxes in my garage and I still haven't found that tape of your mother. It's there somewhere, by golly, but I can't seem to find it."

"Please keep looking." I said. "Let me know if it turns up."

I left the reunion optimistic and determined. I had gotten several tantalizing quotes from my relatives. As a bonus, I had the Hjelm genealogy. I was beginning to put some meat on the bones of my research. And I had a better feel for the land where the old homestead had been.

7
IMMIGRANT DREAMS

Peter's dreams for his American homestead had been modest—to be a lumberman, much as he had been back in Sweden, but now independent, cutting and selling timber grown on his own land. He wasn't a farmer. He didn't particularly want to be a farmer. He had homesteaded this piece of property because it reminded him of home, of Jämtland, only flatter. On these few acres he could do what he wanted to do.

Peter Back was born Pehr Persson Hjelm in the village of Hammarnäs, Sweden, on October 14, 1872, the sixth of fifteen children. Hammarnäs is on the shores of Lake Storsjön across the water from the city of Östersund, even today the only city of any size for hundreds of miles in every direction. Lake Storsjön is large, with over one-hundred-and-seventy square miles of surface, and sits at the geographic center of Jämtland province. The land throughout the region is mountainous with dense forests and clear streams and lakes and only patches of open farmland. Jämtland is the southern edge of the territory where the nomadic Sami people (the Laplanders) once hunted and fished and followed the reindeer herds. Even though Hammarnäs is only seventy miles north of Linsell, where Peter's future wife, Caroline (Lena) Frisk, would be born seven years later, the two weren't to meet until they had traveled thousands of miles on their migration to America.

Peter's mother, Christina Bergstrom Hjelm, was a no-nonsense woman, if it can be said that a mother of fifteen was no-nonsense. Twelve of her children grew to adulthood. Even with his mother's stern countenance, the Hjelm household was always filled with music—thanks primarily to Peter's father, Pehr Anderson Hjelm, my great grandfather.

Pehr Anderson was the oldest son of Anders Hjelm and Stina Martensdotter and at the age of twenty-four had inherited the family farm. But Pehr was more interested in music than in farming. As a teenager he had been smitten with the violin but his father thought the instrument to be the devil's plaything and wouldn't allow his son to have one in the house. Undaunted, Pehr Anderson built his own crude version of a violin and taught himself to play. He eventually took lessons from a local musician, by then having bought a proper instrument. He quickly outgrew his teacher's abilities and began playing at weddings and other socials gatherings. As his reputation grew he became known throughout Jämtland as Hjelm-Pele, the musician.

In his twenties, Hjelm-Pele learned to play the organ. In addition to playing events, he got a job playing the organ in a church in Hallen, a village across a narrow bay of Lake Storsjön from his home in Hammarnäs. Because he owned an organ and the church did not, every Sunday morning Hjelm-Pele would carry his portable Kammerorgel down to his boat, row across the bay to the church, and play for the prayer service. Then he'd pack up and row back home. In the winter he pulled the organ across the ice on a sled. In payment for his first two years as the church's organist he was given half a ton of grain. For thirty-two years he earned a living as a musician, playing at the church and other engagements.

Hjelm-Pele taught three of his sons to play the violin, although not my grandfather, and all the Hjelm children enjoyed music. They would gather to play their instruments and sing and, on occasion, push back the furniture and dance. They sang folk songs and church hymns and danced the schottische and polka and other traditional dances.

As he grew older, Hjelm-Pele eventually got religion and, like his father, came to think of the violin as evil. He felt his three fiddle-playing sons—Marten, Anders, and Olof—had fallen in with other fiddlers of questionable morals and forbid them to play at dances. In true family tradition, however, the boys continued to play; they just didn't tell their father. One evening, Hjelm-Pele walked in on a lively dance where his boys were playing. The music abruptly stopped and a tense quiet filled the room. Hjelm-Pele walked over to Olof and, without a word, took the violin from his hands. He looked at the instrument and snapped on the strings. The three boys were not sure what would happen next. Olof feared his father would smash the instrument.

But after a pause, not sure what he was going to do himself, Hjelm-Pele picked up the bow, set the violin to his chin, and began to tease out a song. After a moment, Marten joined in. Then Anders began to play. Finally, Olof took his second violin, the only one in the family with two, and caught up the tune. Now all the musicians were following Hjelm-Pele's lead, performing for a crowd of enthusiastic dancers. Religious or not, Hjelm-Pele just had to let the music out. All of his sons, including my grandfather, Peter Back, were much the same.

As the middle son, Peter Back's prospects in Sweden were limited. Traditionally, only the oldest son inherited land. More disturbing for Peter, an avowed pacifist, every of-age male faced conscription into the military. Peter felt so strongly that he changed his name from Hjelm, which means helmet, a name with obvious militaristic connotations, to Back, the name of a small hill village near his home. But changing his name didn't improve his prospects. In 1902 he and his brother, Otto, immigrated to America, in the middle of a wave of other Scandinavians. The brothers entered the United States from Canada, making their way to Holmes City, near Alexandria, Minnesota, where several of their relatives had already settled. A year later, Peter and Otto were joined in Holmes City by their father, Hjelm-Pelle, and their mother, Christina.

*Pehr Anderson (Hjelm-Pele) and
Christina Bergstrom Hjelm (Circa 1903)*

Lena Frisk Olson arrived in Holmes City a few months after Peter, in the fall of 1902, and only a few months short of her twenty-third birthday. She was a sight to behold—good looking and slender, with clear blue eyes and a crown of long curly red hair stacked high on her head. She found the town swarming with Swedes—Chellsons, Olsons, Nelsons, and a host of Hjelms, and she and her family were quickly made to feel welcome. Within days of her arrival, Lena and her sisters were working as housekeepers for families in the area.

Lena felt fortunate to find work so quickly with the family of a prominent banker. The job proved to be more than just gainful employment. While working there she met a handsome and charming young man named Peter Back who had been hired to do some handiwork around the house. Two years later Lena and Peter were married.

Peter Persson (Hjelm) and Caroline (Frisk) Back (1904)

The newlyweds moved to Little Falls where Lena was employed by Charles August Lindbergh and his wife Evangeline Lodge Land, parents of two-year-old Charles Lindbergh who, two decades later, was destined to be the first to fly solo nonstop across the Atlantic. Lena liked the house, a large estate overlooking the Mississippi River, with dozens of rooms. But Mrs. Lindbergh was not easy to work for and Lena left her employ shortly before delivering her first child, Elvera (Vera) Christina, born June 20, 1905. Six weeks later, on August 6, the Lindbergh home where Lena had worked burned to the ground.[8]

With a newborn child, Lena and Peter moved back to Holmes City to be closer to their families. Lena was quick to find another job as a housekeeper and Peter found work helping local farmers clear their land. A year and a half later, on December 4, 1906, their second daughter, Clara Linnea, was born.

"It's time we found our own place," Peter said. They both had a burning hope to own their own property.

"Yes," Lena agreed, "but all the good land around here has been claimed. Maybe we should look up north."

Several members of Lena's family had already settled up in Beltrami County, near Upper Red Lake.

"We could take a look up there," Peter suggested, always sensitive to the prevailing winds.

That fall they took the train up to see the area for themselves. Trees and lakes; it was so much like Sweden! They filed their homestead claim in early 1908. Peter cleared a couple of acres and built a simple log cabin.

Back homestead cabin (Circa 1909)

They moved onto the property that winter. The next spring, on April 10, 1909, they had a third daughter, Anna. And on October 21, 1910, a fourth daughter, Hildur, destined to be my mother. By 1913 the Backs were a family of six nestled in a two-hundred-square-foot log cabin on timbered land in Minnesota's far north and living off the land.

8

NO-MAN'S-LAND

The land was theirs, or soon would be, but by 1913 both Lena and Peter already knew they could not make the homestead pay well enough to support their family. In 1908, Peter had gone to the register-of-land office in Bemidji, the Beltrami County Seat. He paid the required ten dollars and filed his affidavit claiming a quarter-section of land in township 153 north, range 30 west, section 5.[9] He committed to build a home on the property, establish his residence there, dig a well, and work the land.

But the Backs, like many homesteaders, did not do as well as they had hoped. The best land had been claimed by earlier settlers. Land near Kelliher opened for homesteading late, not until 1903, after a treaty with the local Red Lake Band of the Anishinaabe Native Americans. But it wasn't good land, the second-growth timber was thin, and they were not one of the first families to file.

Ironically, the land that Peter claimed was almost not included in the United States.

The Backs were among hundreds of thousands of settlers to take advantage of the Homestead Act of 1862 that permitted a U.S. citizen, and those who declared their intent to become a citizen, to claim up to 160 acres of surveyed land.[10] A homesteader was granted ownership if he (women were not included) established residency and worked the land for five years. In 1862 there was a lot of land to give away.

At the end of the Revolutionary War the United States already claimed 890,000 square miles of land extending from the Atlantic Coast westward to the Mississippi River, and from New England south to the Gulf of Mexico, excluding Spanish-held Florida. Then, in 1803, with the Louisiana Purchase, government-owned lands were nearly doubled, reaching westward from the Mississippi to the Rocky Mountains. Ultimately, there were over three-billion square miles of land that would become the forty-eight contiguous states of the union.

But land that Peter Back was to later claim almost ended up in Canada. It would take another fifty years, a series of treaties, and an extensive effort to survey largely uncharted territory, for the United States to acquire the last 30,000 square miles of land that included Peter's claim.

Everyone's seen that little bump on Minnesota's northern border—the Northwest Angle, a surveyor's mistake it appears—that allows Minnesota to claim it's the most northerly state in the lower forty-eight. But that little bump is only the visible part of a much larger miscalculation.

In 1781, the Treaty of Paris set out the eastern boundaries between the U.S. territories to the south and the British Canadian territories to the north.[11] The line ran westward through the Great Lakes to Lake Superior, and from there up the Rainy River, and then, "…through the Lake of the Woods to the northwestern most part thereof, and from thence on a *due west course to the river Mississippi*…"[1*]

But the Mississippi wasn't to the west of Lake of the Woods. The source of the Mississippi, Lake Itasca, was later discovered to be 150 miles *due south*, or 65 miles *south* of where Peter would stake his claim. Lands defined in the Louisiana Purchase were all south of what would become Peter's homestead. What was to become his land was not included in the United States.

It all got straightened out in 1818, except for one noticeable wrinkle: the Northwest Angle. The northern border between the western United States and southern Canada was set at the 49th parallel—a line

---

1 * Emphasis mine

that runs from Puget Sound on the Pacific, 1,300 miles east to Lake of the Woods, where the confusion began—twenty-five miles south of the point agreed to in the Treaty of Paris. To correct the error, the surveyors jogged the border to the north, encompassing Lake of the Woods and the un-surveyed land to the south.[12]

So, forevermore, the Northwest Angle stands as Minnesota's proud claim of northerliness, giving only a begrudging nod to the latecomer, the State of Alaska. And Peter's eventual homestead, Lena and his claim for a better future, finally lay inside the borders of the United States, but—as the Back's were to discover—outside the margins of the Promised Land.

9

CAT-IN-A-HAT

Peter Back took off his boots in the small enclosed porch just outside the cabin door. He stood in his stocking feet as he shook the snow from his fur hat. He looked at the hat in admiration before hanging it on a peg. Lena had made the hat from skins he had cured last fall. It was glossy black with earflaps that could be tied on top of his head if the weather was fine or tied down under his chin if the weather was cold, as it had been today. When he had been in Kelliher earlier in the day, a fellow at the timber yard had looked at his dark mustache and luxurious fur hat and said he looked like a Russian.

Lena had hand-sewn Peter's hat, along with a matching fur shawl for herself, from the skins of a family of black cats that had lived on the homestead the past summer. The queen, already pregnant, had wandered into the yard in the spring of 1913 and birthed and raised her six kittens, also all black, with little human assistance.

While she wouldn't admit it, Lena had occasionally aimed a few squirts into a tin plate when she milked the cow. But she did not, nor did any member of the family consider the feral animals as pets. They were wild creatures, making their living off rodents and birds that fed on kernels of grain spilled when feeding the homestead's livestock. As winter approached, with the pragmatism of a subsistence farmer, Peter harvested the whole clowder, stretching and curing their pelts on wooden frames that he hung in the barn for several weeks.

Peter had worn his fur hat every day this last week as he worked in the woods. The weather had been favorable for cutting timber, cold but clear skies and a light breeze from the northwest. The ground had a good cover of snow, not too deep, and Jim, the ox, was able to drag the logs out of the woods with relative ease. Peter had managed to cut fifty tamarack logs which he sold in town for twenty-five cents apiece. He had taken one load into Kelliher today and he would take four more loads into town over the next two weeks. With ten logs a load, and two dollars and fifty cents or so per trip, Peter figured he'd make a total of twelve or thirteen dollars, about a dollar a day for two weeks of hard labor.

Peter planned to repeat the process in January and maybe a couple of loads in February. If the weather held, he might get another load in March. If he was lucky, Peter figured he could make about fifty dollars before the spring thaw made the road to Kelliher impassable. In July, after the road firmed up, he might be able to sell another couple of wagon-loads before he headed out to North Dakota to work the grain harvest.

Peter, happily singing, pushed open the cabin door. In one hand he held a newspaper. In one coat pocket he had a small bag of candy and in the other pocket, two dollars in coins—the balance of today's earnings after his purchases. The four girls, laughing and squealing, ran to their father and started patting his coat. Anna reached into a pocket and pulled out the bag of candy hidden there.

"After dinner, girls," their mother said.

Dutifully, Anna set the bag of candy down on top of the catalog clippings. Clara reached into her father's other pocket, pulled out the coins and, without a word or a second's hesitation, turned and handed them to her mother. Lena took a jar down from the shelf above the sink, placed the money inside and carefully put the jar back in its place.

Peter hung his coat on a hook by the door, set down the newspaper, and took his usual chair at the head of the table. Vera helped her mother place the bowls and plates of hot food on the table, and then they both sat down to join the others. Before the food was passed, they held hands as Peter said grace. Peter covered his plate with a large helping of mashed potatoes which he topped with venison and green beans. He poured thick venison gravy over all of it. He lathered butter over a thick slice of bread and took a bite. Clara helped Hildur butter her bread and cut her meat into bite-size pieces. Everyone ate quietly with little conversation except an occasional, "Please pass the potatoes," or, "thank you."

When everyone was finished, Vera and Clara cleared the table, putting the leftovers into smaller bowls which they set out on the porch to be kept cold until tomorrow's breakfast or lunch. They stacked the dishes at the end of the sink. Vera took a large enamel coffee pot from the stove and poured steaming water into two dishpans, one for wash, the other for rinse. She began to wash the dishes as Clara took a dishtowel from a hook and prepared to wipe them dry.

Lena retrieved her darning basket from the small closet that was tucked under the stairway leading to the loft and settled into her rocking chair near one of the oil lamps. She pulled out one of Peter's socks and slipped it over a short-handled wooden darning egg. She threaded a needle with yarn similar in color to the sock—*close enough*, she thought—and began to weave a crisscross patch over the hole in the heel. When she finished one stocking, she took another from the basket.

Peter picked up the newspaper he had bought in town and sat down in his rocking chair next to the same oil lamp that Lena was using. Before opening the paper, he withdrew a small, curved tortious shell comb from his shirt pocket and handed it to Lena. "Happy birthday," he said.

Lena was stunned that he'd remembered, and a little miffed that he had spent money so frivolously. Still, her face felt warm and she managed a quiet, "Thank you."

Peter's newspaper was the December 13th issue—the Christmas issue—of the *Svenska Amerikanska Posten*, the *Swedish American Post*, published weekly in Minneapolis and distributed to subscribers throughout the Midwest for one dollar a year. Although it was printed in the Swedish language and had a few articles from the homeland, it mostly covered news of American politics and the doings of other immigrants and immigrant communities. This holiday issue had a drawing of a rag doll, a cut-out that would entertain the girls, and an illustration labeled "Julen 1913" depicting a decorated Christmas tree surrounded by scenes of the holidays—riding on a sleigh, gathering and decorating a tree from the forest, and cooking and serving food for the table. The paper also included several poems and ran the latest installment of a serialized story, advancing the tale by a chapter or two and leaving readers hanging at the end, eager to hear what would happen in the next issue.

Peter scanned the headlines. "It says here that a big storm hit the Great Lakes last month. Over two hundred people were killed and nineteen ships were lost. Others were damaged."

"Do you think that was the big wind that blew through here?" said Lena. "Remember, I remarked about the whistle of the wind around the cabin."

"Could be," Peter replied, as he began to read the article out loud.

Peter's reading was intended mostly for Lena, but he knew the girls were paying close attention as well. Anna and Hildur sat on chairs by the table, their arms wrapped around their legs and their chins resting on their knees. When Vera and Clara finished the dishes they joined their two younger sisters. The older girls pulled their chairs in close, not to miss a word as their father read. He had everyone's full attention as he modulated his voice from deliberate to melodic, adding a bit of drama to each poem and article.

After about an hour, Peter handed the paper to Lena and said to the girls, "Time for bed." Hildur ran over to her father and climbed onto his lap. Before joining her, Anna went and picked up the bag of candy and brought it over to her father. Peter opened the bag and gave each girl one piece of candy—a colorful, chewy gumdrop—and then carefully put the bag in his shirt pocket.

As the girls chewed on the sweets, Peter began to sing a bedtime story, one of his own composition. Sometimes he told Swedish folktales about the adventures of bears and foxes and trolls. At other times he made up songs based on events of the day or about animals in the woods. But tonight his song was about Clara, his second daughter. "Clara was a little girl," he began, as Clara beamed. "She was obedient and strong and a good worker." He had a cheerful note in his voice as he made up the lyrics, telling a story and rhyming the phrases in Swedish.

When Peter finished his song he said, "Off to bed now. Remember, we have the Christmas pageant at school tomorrow."

Without protest, the girls began changing into heavy flannel nightgowns and long stockings. They took turns using the chamber pot set behind the curtain that divided their parent's bed from the rest of the cabin and then washed their hands and brushed their teeth at the kitchen sink. All in a row, they climbed up the steep stairway to the loft. Vera followed behind to give Hildur a needed boost. When the girls reached the upper level, they knelt down around the bed and said in unison: "Now I lay me down to sleep. I pray the Lord my soul to keep. If I should die before I wake, I pray the Lord my soul to take. God bless Mommy, Daddy and all my sisters. Amen."

The section of the stovepipe that ran through the loft no longer glowed, but remained hot to the touch and provided plenty of warmth up under the rafters. Even so, the girls knew it would be cold by morning. They crawled under the thick comforter, two at one end of the bed and two at the other. They were all asleep in minutes. Hildur's last thought as she fell into a dreamless sleep was how nice the mattress smelled, the faint aroma of clover and grass coming from its hay-filled ticking.

As the girls settled in for the night, Peter took a few split pieces of wood from the woodbin and fed them into the stove's firebox. He damped the flue on the stovepipe to keep a low fire going throughout the night. After he extinguished one oil lamp and dimmed the other, he and his wife quietly changed into their nightclothes and prepared for bed, they too saying a quiet prayer before crawling under the bed covers. Like their daughters, they were both asleep within minutes.

The cabin was quiet except for the low hiss of the fire in the stove and the couple's rhythmic breathing. Outside, a few snowflakes floated on the cold night air, weightless and unseen in the forest's impenetrable solitude.

10

COD-SLAB CHRISTMAS

It was a couple of days before Christmas Eve and our house on Dupont Avenue in Minneapolis stank. I was in my mid-teens at the time and greatly offended by the cloying stench of boiling lutefisk that hung heavy in the air.

As was her penchant, Mom had risen an hour before everyone else, made her coffee, and sat down to read the morning paper. With a house full of six kids, she liked to ease into the day, sneaking in a few minutes of quiet solitude. Now mid-morning, she was in the kitchen, standing at the counter.

"What'sha make'n?" I asked.

She looked up at the ceiling when she saw me holding my nose. "Oh, lord," she said, "give me strength."

I was on to her. It was a line she used often, stolen from Victor Mature playing Samson in the 1949 movie *Samson and Delilah*. She had taken me with her to see the film when I was nine or ten. She took me to a lot of movies when I was a kid, mostly Walt Disney films. In exchange, I went with her to see movies she wanted to see—usually a musical or a drama starring some dreamboat like Bing Crosby or Victor Mature or Burt Lancaster.

Although she claimed otherwise, I'm sure she named me Robert Taylor after the popular actor of the era. I hadn't turned out to quite match his handsome countenance. Maybe that's why she taught me this poem:

> I know how ugly I are
> I know my face ain't no star
> But I never mind it
> Because I'm behind it
> The fellow out front gets the jar.

She never taught it to any of my siblings—why was that I wonder?

The movies were an enchanting escape for her and for me. I routinely spent half of my fifty-cents-a-week allowance going to the Saturday matinee at the nearby Boulevard Theater—five cartoons, a serial, and the feature—all for twenty-five cents plus a nickel for a treat. The balance of my allowance I spent on ten-cent comic books. When I got a little older, I'd take the streetcar downtown to see a horror film—Dracula, Frankenstein, and the like—sometimes with a titillating anthropological short featuring bare-breasted African natives, a bit of movie theater "educational" chicanery to get around the censors.

Anyway, back in the kitchen, Mom went back to her work, shaking her head. "I'm making Swedish meatballs," she answered. "Here, wash your hands and you can lend a hand. And quit acting like a baby."

It was the same every Christmas. For a couple of days before we gathered, the house reeked with the smell of lutefisk—a Scandinavian tradition that should have died there. Lutefisk is cod that has been preserved in lye, a process that makes it impervious to hurricanes, locusts, and marauding animals. In its dormant state, a slab of lutefisk is as stiff as a hardwood plank but less appetizing. To make it edible, the slab needs to be soaked in water for days then boiled to a gelatinous consistency that resembles a dead jellyfish. It is served to those who dare with white-sauce and butter.

"These are for you," she said, as she rolled a spoonful of meat in the palms of her hands. She placed the meatball—a little smaller than a ping-pong ball—on a piece of waxed paper. "They're for you and the other cowards in the family."

"Why do you make that stinky stuff?" I asked, as I added another meatball to the growing collection.

"I like it," she said. "And it's part of the Back tradition."

Years later I read somewhere that people in Sweden considered lutefisk an old-fashioned food for the poor and desperate. Some thought the Vikings had invented the diabolical method of preserving fish so they could use the indestructible slabs to club to submission those they vandalized on their legendary plundering voyages and then have something to eat at the victory celebration. No self-respecting modern Scandinavian would deign to partake of the stuff. But each Christmas, with dogged determination, my mother served it. She either liked it or she liked the memories that wafted in its miasma.[2][*13]

When I was young, in the days leading up to the holidays, Mother would take us kids to Dayton's department store in downtown Minneapolis. First we'd walk along the street gazing at the elaborately decorated windows—sleighs filled with gaily wrapped packages with bright ribbons, elves with hammers and saws assembling toys in Santa's workshop, and ornately decorated Christmas trees with kids opening presents. Often the windows told a story, each window a scene in the storyline. With mounting excitement, we'd ride the escalator up to the top floor where the store had created a Santa-land labyrinth that culminated at Santa's workshop and a chance to sit on the jolly elf's lap and tell him what special gift we wanted for Christmas.

Mom hosted Christmas Eve at the family home for decades. Mom and Dad purchased the house, a two-story colonial with four bedrooms, when my brother Steve was born, their fourth child with more anticipated. The house had a large dining room that could seat ten or twelve and a spacious living room where, for the Christmas Eve dinner, we kids bonded with our cousins as we ate at a couple of card tables, frequently glancing in eager anticipation at all the gifts tucked under the sparkling Christmas tree.

Before dinner, Mom set out a pitcher of warm cranberry juice mixed with tea and spiced with orange and cinnamon, bottles of vodka and brandy, and an array of glass tea cups. The dinner menu didn't vary much from year to year: Swedish meatballs with gravy (for years Mom ground her own mix of pork and beef until I could drive

---

2   *Instructions on how to enjoy lutefisk can be found in the End Notes.

and she sent me out to a suburban grocery that carried a pre-mix, a twenty mile round trip that made my fledgling driver's heart sing), mashed potatoes, baked creamed corn, homemade cranberry sauce with orange zest, and that ubiquitous green-bean casserole baked in Campbell's mushroom soup and topped with crispy onions. My favorite was warm homemade Parker House rolls dripping with butter. And, of course, there was a platter of lutefisk.

When I finished eating, I'd leave my seat at the card table and wander into the dining room to listen in on the conversation, standing at the fringes of that animated gathering of adults. I thought I was big stuff when I was finally invited to eat with the others around that long dining table.

The guest list varied over the years but often included whatever members of our extended family happened to be in town—an uncle or aunt from my mother's side or my dad's cousin and his wife. As we kids got older with spouses and kids of our own the number of guests could easily expand to twenty-five of more. Whatever the size, the crowd didn't seem to rattle my mom—but then little did. "There's always room for one more," she said, "if you're willing to share." She was always ready for unexpected guests, holidays or not. In the basement she kept a second refrigerator stocked with cheap Champagne, just in case something or someone needed celebrating.

When we finished rolling the meatballs, Mom began to brown them in a large cast iron skillet. Later, she'd stir in flour with the juices to make a thick roux and then thin it with beef stock to make rich gravy.

"That smells good," I said, as the meatballs sizzled in the pan. "It sure smells better than that damn fish."

She picked up a knife from the counter and turned to me with an exaggerated scowl on her face. "Mind your language or I'll wash out your mouth with soap," she said as she brought the knife to her apron, point up. "Now, get out of my kitchen or I'll cut your guts out." I think she picked up that line, or at least the attitude, from James Cagney, probably from the movie *Love Me or Leave Me* with Doris Day. She'd taken me to that one too. Mom was the farthest one could get from being a drama queen, but occasionally she'd show a little bit of theater.

"June Allison wouldn't say that," I said.

She lifted the tip of the knife. "Get out," she growled.

"I need to set a fire in the fireplace," I said, and kissed her on the cheek.

After Christmas Eve dinner, my dad would escape to the sunroom to read the paper, take a nap, or (when we got one) watch a little television. He enjoyed the conversation at the table but was overwhelmed with the din and chaos that followed. One year my niece, Annie, then about six, sneaked into the room and fiddled with the TV remote while she watched in awe as her grandfather ate an apple, the whole thing, core and all. She asked him, "Won't the seeds grow a tree?" He looked at her thoughtfully and replied, "I suppose if you add dirt." He wiped his chin and held out his hand. "Give me the remote," he said, having had enough of her incessant use of the zoom button.

Glen Vivian Taylor (Circa 1942)

After the tables had been cleared, everyone—including my dad—spread out around the Christmas tree which was decorated with an eclectic assortment of glass balls and ornaments, a string of bubbling candle lights, and (everyone's favorite) a long garland of small lighted oriental lanterns. Over everything, the tree was festooned with strands of glittering silver tinsel.

The base of the tree was encircled by a mountain range of brightly wrapped packages reaching three feet into the room. The younger children took turns passing out the gifts. To keep the number of gifts within a semblance of propriety, the adults drew each other's names. But there was no holding back on gifts for the kids—Christmas is, after all, a celebration of the earthly promise of every newborn, of every child.

Later in the evening, several of us joined Mom at Mount Olivet Lutheran Church for one of the services in their Christmas Eve marathon. I have to admit, the music was glorious and the sermon short. One year, when I was a teenager, the church added a new twist. As the sermon progressed, a stained-glass larger-than-life image of Jesus became visible behind the pulpit. His beatific face and welcoming arms gradually became brighter, reaching full illumination just as the minister reached the climax of his sermon. I'm sure it inspired many impressionable youth to pursue the ministry. I know I was dazzled and I was eager to see it again. The next year, however, the Christ image snapped on from black to bright with the flip of a switch. *What happened to the subtleness of the year before? Did the rheostat break?* Shallow as I was, I went home a cynic. It was one more disillusionment contributing to my slide into heresy.

When I was young and still a believer, Santa came to our home at night, unseen, after we kids were asleep. Before we went to bed, we would make sure the ashes in the fireplace were cold. More than once I remember smoothing out the ashes in the hope that I'd catch Santa's footprints. One special Christmas morning, when I was seven, I found a full-sized bicycle—an orange-colored JC Higgins with a fork tank and built-in horn, fenders, and a silver bullet headlight—waiting for me by the fireplace. The bike was too big for my short legs, so for a couple of years I rode it without the saddle, rocking the bike left and right so my feet could reach the peddles.

From everything I knew, it was clear that my mother put a great deal of stock in Christmas. But where did that love for the holiday start? What had Christmas been like up at the homestead cabin when she was a child? By the time I even thought of that question it was too late. Mother's memory was beginning to slip. When I tried to interview her about her childhood, she was able to confirm a few vignettes I fed back to her, stories I had remembered from years past. But she could not enhance any of the tales or add any details. Her brother Glenn never lived at the cabin, so I turned my attention to her sisters. First, I focused on my Aunt Ann.

Ann was the third oldest of the five sisters: Elvera (Vera), the oldest, then Claire (Clara), Ann (Anna), my mother Hildur, and Sally (Selma). The youngest, her brother Glenn, followed the female covey by ten years. I knew Aunt Ann as a strong, gregarious and energetic woman. When I was growing up, Ann lived on a farm near Bemidji where she raised five of my cousins, all boys, with her husband Oscar Stennes. When Oscar died she went back to school and became a teacher. In her later years she was a socially active dynamo. And, to my surprise and delight, she had researched and written an historical article on the family for her local newspaper. She sent me a copy in preparation for my interview.

Ann Sophia Back Stennes (2000)

She was ninety years old and undiminished when I called her on the telephone, tape recorder at hand.

"You know," she said, "we were rich in so many ways we didn't know we were poor. I remember, especially, a Christmas at the cabin when I was still quite young…"

11

BARREL MINISTRY

Anna awoke from a sound sleep to the smell of coffee. The sleeping loft was in shadow except for the faint glow of an oil lamp rising through the hole in the floor where the steep steps led downstairs. She lay in bed, the comforter pulled up to her chin, her eyes peering at where the dim light shown on the rafters only a few feet above her head. Webs of fine silvery frost clung to the underside of the roof boards. She could see individual crystals, some with feathery edges like the lace on Mama's best apron, the one she wore when guests were in the house. As the stovepipe began to heat, she knew the delicate feathers would start to lose their shape. Before she finished breakfast the frost would all be gone.

Peter had told the girls that today would be a big day, a Christmas pageant at school. Hildur, only three, couldn't remember Christmas from last year and was uncertain what a pageant was, but her sisters had been talking about it for several days. She guessed it was a party and she knew what that was. There would be singing and good food and Vera had said a tree would be inside the school. *A tree inside?* Hildur had to see that. And Clara had said there would be gifts for everybody. Hildur couldn't help being excited.

Vera was already up and dressed and downstairs helping Mama. Clara gave each of her sisters a poke and said, "Get up lazybones!"

When Anna and Hildur were out of bed and dressed, Clara led the two down the stairway, making sure both younger girls made it safely on the steep incline. Anna and Hildur were both quite secure on the stairs and Anna was beginning to resent Clara's protectiveness and poked her in the back when they got to the bottom. "Hurry up slowpoke," she mimicked Clara's instructions.

The breakfast table was already set with a glass of milk by each place setting, a pitcher of sweet cream, a bowl filled with freshly churned butter, and a basket of sliced jule kake—a sweet holiday bread Lena made with raisins, ground cardamom, and pieces of dried fruit when she could find them.[14]

Vera took two platters from the warming oven above the stove, one with a dozen fried eggs and the other heaped with fried potatoes, and placed them on the table. After saying grace, Peter took three eggs for his plate and a generous scoop of potatoes and then passed the platters around for others to take their share. He picked up a slice of bread, spread on a thick layer of butter, and dipped a corner into the soft yoke of one of the eggs. He and the others ate quietly but with enthusiasm and obvious appreciation.

When Peter finished he poured a cup of coffee for Lena and one for himself. Outside, dawn was just beginning to lighten the sky. Peter blew across the top of his coffee cup and reached for a small bowl of sugar cubes that Lena had put on the table. He placed a sugar cube on his tongue and took a sip of coffee. He sat forward in his chair, resting his elbows on the table. Lena gave him a look as she pushed a sugar cube under her lip. Peter eased back in his chair and slipped his offending elbows off the table. Clutching his cup in both hands, he said, "The preacher from Holmes City will stop by later this morning, I gave him a lift from Kelliher yesterday and dropped him off at the Olson's for the night. He'll stay with the Chellson's tonight, after the pageant."

"He's always welcome to stay with us," Lena said. They often had overnight guests at the cabin, some friend or relative passing through. Everyone they knew did the same. Sometimes the guest would sleep in the loft with the girls or downstairs on the floor near the back wall.

"I offered him our place," Peter said," but he wanted to see the Olsons first. Maybe he had something at the top of his barrel for them."

Reverend Johnson always came to visit just before Christmas. He was a Baptist missionary who traveled from one Swedish settlement to another, covering a score of small communities throughout northern Minnesota.[15] Lena thought he chose to come to this remote part of the state because so many up here had relatives back in Holmes City. He traveled without any means of his own transportation, no horse, no sleigh. He moved about by train on occasion, but mostly he hitched a ride with a local farmer, as he had with Peter. His visits were always welcome. He was a pleasant and soft-spoken man who brought news of what other Swedes were doing: who was getting married, who had a baby, and who had died. He wasn't a powerful speaker but his sermons were thoughtful and comforting.

Peter knew Reverend Johnson thought card playing and dancing were sinful but he had a kind heart. He didn't shake his finger at people or preach hell-and-damnation like some others of his kind. He wasn't at all arrogant and Peter suspected he had sinned a little in his past and didn't feel too far above the simple peasants he considered his flock. Besides, he brought a guitar along on his travels and had a nice singing voice. Peter looked forward to a little music at the pageant.

Lena had another reason to welcome Reverend Johnson. He always brought a wooden barrel packed tight with used clothing that had been collected by the Baptist and Lutheran churches in Holmes City. The barrel contained all sorts of surprises: old coats, dresses, pants, shoes and hats. Often: stockings, mittens or gloves. Sometimes a piece of clothing or a pair of shoes actually fit, but mostly Lena looked for items that were made of good quality material that she could alter or mend to fit some member of the family.

After announcing Reverend Johnson's expected arrival, Peter said, "Before lunch we'll be going to the school for the Christmas pageant." When he finished his announcement he sat back and continued to sip his coffee. As Vera and Clara cleared the table and prepared to wash the dishes, Lena moved over to her pedal-driven sewing machine. The morning light was now strong enough that she could get in an hour of productive work before assembling her contributions to the pageant's smorgasbord.

When he finished his coffee, Peter got up from the table, put on his hat, coat and boots and stepped outside to do his morning chores.

Mid-morning, Peter came into the house carrying a large wood-staved barrel. Behind him came Reverend Johnson carrying his travel bag, and on his back, a guitar wrapped and tied in a woolen blanket. The pastor was a head shorter than Peter but solidly built; broad at the shoulders and long-waisted. His legs were short even for a man of his diminutive stature and Peter had joked to Lena that if they were any shorter they wouldn't reach the ground. Lena had given Peter a stern look and he hadn't repeated his joke, but he rather liked the image of a holy man levitating serenely an inch or two above the earth.

Peter set the barrel down next to the table and turned to take Reverend Johnson's bag and placed it near the bottom of the stairway. The reverend greeted Lena with a "God Jule" and a warm smile. He did not extend his hand nor did she extend hers. To each of the children he gave another "God Jule," greeted them by name and gave each a piece of hard candy.

"Thank you," said Hildur. *Two days and two pieces of candy. I like Christmas!*

"Welcome Reverend," said Lena. "Let's sit down. I have coffee and some cinnamon rolls."

With Reverend Johnson at the table there was an unusual amount of conversation between sips of coffee and bites of food, with the pastor doing most of the talking. He told of his recent visit to a Swedish couple who lived near Little Falls, where Lena and Peter had worked several years earlier. "Lena, you knew the woman when she worked for the Lindbergh's, didn't you?" the reverend asked. Lena nodded. "She also left the Lindbergh's and now works for another family, the Nelsons. She and her husband recently had another boy, their fourth child, Nels. I officiated at the baby's christening. The father is a good man, a hard worker."

Reverend Johnson continued his report of the news, always careful not to reveal any confidences or to interject his judgments, unless they were favorable. Neither Peter nor Lena asked many questions or made comment. They just listened and nodded. The reverend continued almost as if he had a script, as perhaps he did. During his many hours alone, traveling from one community to another, he thought carefully about what would interest his parishioners and what might be perceived as an intrusion. Members of his Swedish flock were curious but were quick to draw a line if they thought someone was revealing matters better left private. After all, people didn't want the reverend telling stories about them to strangers or, worse yet, to people they knew. Peter and Lena thought Reverend Johnson knew the difference between news and gossip.

When the reverend finished his news and the table was cleared, he said, "Let's look in my barrel and see what we can find."

Although she didn't reveal her feelings, Lena was as excited as the children to see what the barrel might contain. She watched as the reverend opened the snap on the metal band that encircled the barrel's lid. He removed the band and lifted off the round top and laid it aside. He untied a heavy cord from around the folds of an oilcloth bag that lined the barrel's interior and started removing items, carefully laying each piece out on the surface of the now bare table. The aroma of cedar chips tickled Anna's nose.

As the reverend pulled out a linen dress, Lena noted that it was much too large for her. Still, the material was unsoiled and of good quality, with a row of buttons on the bodice and a wide lace collar. *I could make a fine Sunday dress from that*, she thought. The dress was followed by a child's coat of green wool plaid that proved to fit Clara just right. Lena thought the material was sturdy enough to last until Anna grew into it, maybe even Hildur.

Reverend Johnson continued to withdraw items from the barrel until Lena had selected one article for each member of the family. In addition to the dress for herself and the coat for Clara, Lena selected a wool sweater that buttoned down the front for Vera. For Peter, she chose a pair of wide, blue suspenders, and for Hildur, a pair of long woolen stockings. Anna was especially delighted to get a pair of black patent-leather shoes, with a button on the heel, even though they were a little too large. Lena thought Anna would grow into them by spring.

"They're just like the ones in the catalog!" Anna squealed and jumped down from her chair with the shoes in hand. She ran over to the sink and with her index finger placed a dab of butter on the toe of each shoe. She started polishing with the corner of a dishtowel. Lena quietly removed the dishtowel from Anna's hand and gave her a rag from under the kitchen sink. Over the next few weeks Anna would polish and re-polish those shoes at least a dozen times.

Lena expected Reverend Johnson to close the barrel—they had already received more than she expected. Instead, the reverend reached deep down along an inside edge of the barrel. He pulled out a book and handed it to Lena. "This is a special gift for you," he said. It was a book on European history, in Swedish. "Your relatives in Holmes City know how much you enjoy reading history. It's from the library. You can return it next time you visit."

Lena was nearly speechless. "Thank you. I've read so little lately."

"I can read it to you," Peter interjected, "while you're darning my socks."

Lena smiled and nodded her head. "Please thank the people back in Holmes City for me," she said, as she pushed back a lock of hair from her forehead.

Peter noted that Reverend Johnson had not drawn more than a couple of extra items out of the barrel before he had found something for every member of the family—and now the book. *He must arrange things in there before he ever leaves Holmes City*, he thought.

In fact, the good reverend tried. He knew his flock well and selected items he thought would be appropriate and then laid them in the barrel so the articles he'd need first would be on top. He didn't always guess as well as he did with the Backs, but he usually came close. He also packed a few wool blankets along the sides of the bag so he could quickly pull one out if he guessed wrong. A good wool blanket was always welcome. If it wasn't needed for a bed, an industrious housewife could make a pair of sturdy work pants or a jacket for her husband or warm coats for her children. There would still be scraps of material left over that could be made into mittens, gloves, a hat, or some other useful item.

"You'll ride with us to the school?" Peter asked. "It's the Christmas pageant."

"Yes, please," the reverend said as he resealed the barrel. "I've been looking forward to it."

12

HOMESTEADER'S HOLIDAY

Anna watched her breath plume white against the bright sky. The air was crisp and she could feel a prickly breeze against her cheeks as the horse drew the sled along the narrow cut that led from the main road through the woods to the schoolhouse. The sound of the horse's hooves was muffled by the snow, with an occasional clop, clop, as they hit a patch of hard-pack or ice. The sled's runners made a soft shushing sound that reminded her of the whistling she heard in the cabin's eaves when the wind came up during the night.

Anna sat huddled with her mother and sisters on top of a wool blanket that had been laid over several inches of hay spread across the sled's wooden flatbed. They were loosely wrapped in a couple of puffy comforters, more to protect them from the breeze than from the cold itself. If they had been standing still they would have been comfortably warm in their layers of cotton and wool. Peter stood at the front of the sled, the reins in his mittened hand and his black fur hat perched on his head, the flaps tied up. Unusually, he was not singing, in deference to Reverend Johnson who sat next to him. The reverend's short legs dangled over the sled's leading edge, his feet well above the snow passing beneath. His guitar lay just behind him, still wrapped in its protective blanket. His barrel of Christmas goodies was tied down near the back, ready to be transferred to the sled of his next visitation.

It was two miles from the cabin to the schoolhouse, a run of a mile and a half straight west on the county road and then a sharp right north for another half mile, over Domaas creek to the shores of Upper Red Lake. Ordinarily they would have walked, especially on a clear day like today. But they had Reverend Johnson, and his barrel, and the food, and other packages. In addition to food for the smorgasbord, Lena had made extra loaves of jule kake she intended to give away as gifts. They were also bringing items for the children's gift exchange, one for each child, all wrapped together in a dishcloth along with strings of pinecones and popcorn, and paper-chains the children had made from strips of old newspaper glued together with a flour and water paste. An eight-foot balsam tree was tied down at the back of the sled. Peter had used scrap lumber to create a cross-board stand that would keep the tree upright.

As they came to the turn in the road, Peter slowed the horse to a near standstill. The horse knew the way, but Peter was careful to take the corner slow and wide to be sure the sled didn't drop a runner into the deep drainage ditch that paralleled the roadway.

The last half-mile was Anna's favorite part of the ride, a narrow cut through thick trees, the branches brushing the sides of the sled as they glided through. As they neared the lake the trees gave way to a wind-swept clearing with a small square building set back about two hundred feet from the lakeshore. Between the schoolhouse and the lake, snow had drifted into dunes, piled eight feet high and honeycombed with tunnels dug by industrious school children playing Eskimo during recess. Other sleds and horses were already there, children throwing snowballs and parents talking quietly as they filed into the school building.

Peter reined in the horse at the schoolhouse door. As Lena and the girls climbed down from the sled, Peter and Reverend Johnson untied the tree and carried it inside the building.

The schoolroom had been cleared of furniture, the student desks stacked along one wall. In one corner of the room stood a large potbellied stove, a glint of yellow flames visible through a mica panel in its door, its cast iron shell creaking and groaning as it gained heat. A two-tiered metal rack encircled the stove, draped with an assortment of hats, mittens, and coats wet from the snow.

At the tree's peak Peter fastened a metal star he had cut and shaped from an empty two-pound coffee can. Then he and Reverend Johnson stood the tree upright on its base. They placed the tree in the opposite corner from the stove and well away from the doorway. That way, Peter reasoned, if there was a fire everybody could still get out without having to get past the tree. As they secured the tree in place, Ole Olson, Peter's brother-in-law, came in carrying two full buckets of water he'd drawn from the lake through a hole he'd chopped in the foot-thick ice. He set the buckets down next to the tree, the balsam's lush green branches reaching out into the room, ready now for decorating.

Lena and the other women began to put food on two long rough-hewn planks laid between the teacher's table and a couple of the larger student desks pushed back against one wall. For a poor community, the rich array of foods was impressive. Two large bowls of mashed potatoes, a large tureen of white gravy, a platter of deviled eggs, and a large thick-sliced ham adorned the makeshift table. Three kinds of bread—Lena's jule kake, a rye limpa, and a basket of hot-cross-buns—warmed by the stove. Ginger snaps, delicate rings of kransekaker, plump prune-filled kolaches, and Lena's favorite—light and buttery spritz—were mounded on platters. The scent of balsam filled the room, mixed with the aromas of coffee and hot chocolate steaming from large enamel pots heating on the stove.

As often happened, Peter had been asked to serve as the pageant's master-of-ceremonies. He was comfortable in front of an audience and usually had something appropriate or funny to say. He now stood near the tree and in a loud voice said, "Welcome to the Christmas pageant! It is a pleasure for me to welcome again Reverend Harold Johnson from Holmes City who will lead us in a prayer."

Reverend Johnson was well known to everyone in the room but he nevertheless appreciated the introduction. He led the gathering in a simple prayer of thanks and when he finished the crowd responded with a collective "Amen" and let loose on the awaiting food. As people filled their plates, the reverend unwrapped his guitar and tuned the strings as best he could given the instrument's regular exposure to an extreme range of temperatures. When he was satisfied, he sat on a low stool and strummed a few basic cords as he began to sing. With his pleasant tenor voice, he started with a couple familiar Swedish hymns and then moved to a selection of well-known Christmas carols. Peter was the first to join the reverend in singing "Silent Night." Lena added her clear soprano and soon nearly everyone in the room had joined the chorus.

After singing several carols, Peter whispered to Reverend Johnson that it was time to play "Oh Little Town of Bethlehem." The reverend strummed his guitar and hummed the melody as Peter began to read aloud the Christmas story from a small bible he'd brought from home: "In those days Caesar Augustus issued a decree that a census should be taken…"

As Peter continued to read and Reverend Johnson's song reached its second chorus, Vera walked forward arm-in-arm with her ten-year-old cousin, Otto. Vera's head was covered with a blue shawl and she carried in her arms a doll wrapped in a dishcloth. Otto had another dishtowel wrapped around his head as a turban. The holy couple sat down on the floor in front of the tree, beneath the coffee-can star, trying to look solemn instead of just nervous. Other children began to file in from both sides, one beating earnestly on a small drum, another carrying a cigar box filled, no doubt, with frankincense and myrrh. Two other children carried pine boughs, and two others, paper cutouts of sheep.

When the pageant had finished the crowd applauded generously. As if on signal, strings of pinecones and popcorn, paper-chains, and paper cutout birds and stars magically appeared from coat pockets and packages and were strung in draping garlands from the tree's boughs. Small unwrapped gifts, a few tied with string or ribbon, but most unadorned, were placed under the tree. Lastly, Peter and Ole Olson securely tied a dozen white candles to the ends of carefully selected branches. They then slipped a paper circle over each candle, pushing it down to the candle's base to catch any wax drippings. When all was ready, Reverend Johnson began to play and sing "O Tannenbaum" as Peter lit each candle. Ole stood next to the water pails trying to look nonchalant but obviously a little apprehensive, alert to the possibility of fire and ready to throw a bucket of water if needed.

When the candles were all lit, Peter looked at Ole and then at the crowd. "Ole looks as nervous as a black cat in my farmyard," he joked, as he twirled his fur hat on his hand.

The oil lamps were dimmed and the room glowed softly in the flickering candlelight. Reverend Johnson led the crowd in two choruses of "Silent Night" and then a prayer of thanksgiving. After a moment of silence the candles on the tree were snuffed out, one by one, and the oil lamps turned back up to full illumination. The light outside was already beginning to fade and with little fanfare the children exchanged gifts.

Then it was over. Decorations were removed from the tree, dishes and gifts packed away, and the children bundled again in their leggings, heavy coats and wool caps. Families began to depart, wishing each other, "God Jule."

Peter and Ole, with the aid of a couple of other men, put the student furniture back in its place, damped the stove, and hauled out the tree.

Anna sat on the sled bundled under warm blankets with her mother and sisters waiting for her father to close up the school. It wouldn't be opened again until after New Year's. She looked out across the frozen expanse of Upper Red Lake. Patches of ice glowed golden as the sun perched on the distant horizon. It wasn't a sight she saw often. Usually the sun disappeared into the trees, its last rays reflected in the sky.

The light was fading quickly as the horse followed the road back to the homestead. Peter lit the oil lamp he kept on the sled and Anna watched its soft light dance off pine boughs and tree branches that emerged from the shadows to sweep past them, disappearing again into the darkening forest. Anna looked up and saw the first stars of the evening. As if on cue, Peter said, "Star light, star bright, first star I see tonight. I wish I will, I wish I might, have the wish I wish tonight." Anna and her sisters stared into the heavens. Anna wasn't sure what she should wish for. The day had been a delight. She had seen her cousins and gotten two gifts today, she still had one piece of hard candy hidden in her pocket, and now she was doing one of her favorite things, riding on the sled at night. "*This* is what I wish for," she thought.

As they reached the cabin, a bright canopy of uncountable stars lit the heavens. "Look," Anna said, "I can see the Milky Way!"

13

LOG-CABIN YULE

It was Christmas Eve and Lena, as always, was the first one in the house to awake in the morning. She slipped out from under the covers and lit an oil lamp, damping the wick so there was just enough light to move about without tripping over something. She went behind the curtained partition that separated the bed from the rest of the cabin, lifted her nightgown and squatted over the chamber pot. When she was finished she took the large enamel teapot that was always on the stove and poured warm water into a washbasin. She wet a sponge in the basin, rubbed it across a bar of soap, and gave herself a quick sponge bath, washing only the critical areas, before getting dressed. Saturday was the day everyone in the family took a real bath. Friday night, before going to bed, Lena would bring in water from the well, or better yet, soft water from the rain barrel if it wasn't frozen, and put a pot on the stove so there would be plenty of warm water when she and Peter took their baths in the morning before the children awoke. After the two adults had bathed, Lena would heat more water for the children. They were given their baths after breakfast, after Peter went out for chores and before Lena started preparations for lunch.

As Lena started breakfast, Peter continued to sleep. She didn't begrudge him his extra few minutes of rest. He often got up in the night to add a log or two to the stove and, in truth, these few quiet minutes in the morning were one of her only moments of solitude in her busy day..

Today her family would celebrate Christmas and, even though she had started preparations well in advance, she still had much to do. Most of the gifts that would be passed out after dinner this evening she had been working on for weeks, sewing dresses for the girls from the bolt of cloth she'd gotten from the Wards catalog last fall.

She had started cooking in earnest this last Monday, December 22, her birthday. Lena had not expected her birthday to be much different from any other day, and it hadn't been. Except for the surprise gift from Peter and, perhaps, there had been even more work to do than usual.

Defrosting the lutefisk for Christmas Eve dinner was one task that had needed doing that day. Sunday afternoon she had gone out to the barn to retrieve the slab of dried lutefisk Peter had purchased at the mercantile in Kelliher. The long white fillet had been frozen and she had felt it was best kept that way until she was ready for it. Not that it would have been any less solid had it been allowed to thaw. Along Sweden's coast, drying fish with lye was a traditional way of preserving it for storage and shipping to inland farmers, like salting pork or smoking ham. The fillet had been kept in the house overnight, white as snow, leaning against the stairway across from the kitchen stove. By Monday morning it had thawed but was still stiff as a board. To prepare the fish for cooking she needed to remove the lye preservative. She had placed the fillet in the laundry tub and covered it with cold water. Each morning since, she had replaced the water and continued to let the fish soak. This afternoon she would boil the softened fillet for an hour or so, filling the cabin with its strong acidic aroma. When it was served in the evening, the lutefisk would be translucent, nearly transparent. Lena would cut it into squares and serve it hot, with a creamy white sauce poured over the top and melted butter on the side.

The week before, Lena had made several kinds of Christmas cookies and had expanded her selection even further by exchanging with other housewives at the school pageant. She had baked additional loaves of jule kake and limpa. After breakfast she would bring in potatoes from the abundant supply stored in the root cellar, and a jar of canned vegetables, green beans she thought. And a jar of strawberry preserves. There would be plenty to eat.

That afternoon, Peter brought a balsam tree into the house. It was the top six feet of the tree he'd used for the pageant, trimmed smaller for the cabin, with the same crossed-board stand nailed to its new base and the same coffee-can star fixed to its top. As he had done at the school, he stood the tree opposite the door, between the bed and the back wall.

As Lena put the lutefisk on the stove to boil, Peter and the girls decorated the tree with the same garlands they had used at the school. As before, Peter tied a number of white candles on carefully selected branches and placed a bucket of water near the door. When the tree was decorated, Lena arranged a few packages at its base, each gift wrapped in old copies of the *Swedish American Post* and tied with string.

The girls thought eating dinner would take forever. They liked the food, but they were eager for their father to light the candles on the tree and excited to open their presents. Hildur had been delighted with the Christmas pageant at school and now knew what to expect. All during the meal the girls' eyes kept glancing toward the tree and the presents beneath. Vera was eager for everyone to finish eating so she could clear the table.

Finally, when the meal was finished and the dishes were washed and put away, the entire Back family gathered on the floor around the Christmas tree while Peter lit the candles. Hildur thought the tree was even more beautiful than the one at school. She stared into the twinkling lights as her father and mother sang a favorite hymn. Later, as she lay in bed slipping into a child's untroubled sleep, the twinkle of a hundred candles danced behind her closed eyelids.

14

RESILIENT AND DETERMINED

"So," I said to my Aunt Claire, who was then ninety-three, "what do you remember most about living in a log cabin?"

Sue and I had invited Claire to join us for lunch in a quiet Minneapolis restaurant where we could talk. I placed a small cassette recorder in the middle of the table.

Claire was the second oldest of the Back sisters and had always been brave and resourceful. In an earlier interview, she had told me about some of her adventures. When she was twenty-one, she and a girlfriend hitched a ride from Minneapolis to Los Angeles—a seven-day drive in a Chevrolet coup driven by a guy they didn't know and who was insensitive to their needs. "He never stopped for us," said Claire. "There weren't many service stations like they have now. We were so bashful we wouldn't ever tell him we needed to go to the bathroom. We just suffered, we needed to go so badly."

They arrived in Los Angeles in September, 1928, just a year before the start of the Great Depression. They got work immediately at Bullox, a big department store in downtown Los Angeles. "Every department had a clerk," Claire said. "Customers didn't help themselves. I was in blouses and lingerie."

She was laid off after Christmas but wasn't worried. She was also an experienced waitress and got a job at the Pig and Whistle, a popular restaurant chain at the time. Later, she followed another friend to a Pig and Whistle in Hollywood, directly across from Grumman's Chinese Theater. "We had fun," Claire told me. "We met a lot of movie stars and waited on them. I met Al Jolson…and other celebrities you don't even know."

"When the depression hit, we were naïve, we didn't even know what a depression was. We kept working as waitresses. We didn't make a lot of money. We got our food and we got our salary, which wasn't very much, but our rent was cheap. For a while we had an apartment right under that big Hollywood sign up on the hill, the one you see on all the postcards."

"Then we applied for work at a resort up at Lake Tahoe. We went swimming in the lake. We went horseback riding. We hitched a ride to Reno. That was one of the nicest summers of my whole life. Then the manager of the resort asked me if I'd like to work the winter at the Biltmore just outside Phoenix."

Claire Linnea Back at Lake Tahoe (Circa 1930)

"We jumped around like that. We'd work the season, then get a waitress job for a few weeks between seasons, then back to a resort. We were never out of work. Then, in 1932, I came home, back to Minneapolis."

Not long after her return, Claire and my mother roomed together, sharing macaroni and cheese dinners, the only two sisters to live in Minneapolis. Years later, Claire and her husband, Roy Porter, lived not far from my parents. Their son, my cousin Tom, was just a year younger than me and we were frequent playmates and best of friends.

From early childhood to our early teens, Tom and I spent our summers up at Hall's Moose Lake Resort. Elvera and Delbert Hall had been married in 1925 and bought the resort in the early 1940s.

Elvera and Delbert Hall (1925)

Del taught us to bait a hook and clean fish, how to use a rifle safely and shoot straight, how to split wood and build a fire, how to row a boat and use an outboard motor, and how to churn ice cream. Every week or so, he would take us with him into Bemidji. He'd drop us at Paul Bunyan, on the shores of Lake Bemidji, while he ran errands. Tom and I entertained ourselves while he was gone, hiking along the lakeshore or visiting a small museum that collected authentic Paul

Bunyan artifacts, including, among others, a six-foot steel pike purported to be Paul's toothpick.

When Del picked us up he would take us to a soda fountain where we each had our own chocolate malt mixed in a steel canister. "They're made right," he told us, "when the straw stands up in the middle."

Elvera taught us how to find and pick wild berries, how to cook fish (dredged in flour and fried in butter with a little onion), how to snag a chicken by the leg, tuck its head under a wing to calm it down, wring its neck, then chop off its head while keeping all our fingers. She taught us the importance of doing our chores.

On more than one moonless night, Elvera and Del would invite us outside into the inky dark to gaze at the star-filled heavens and the bright swath of the Milky Way. Once or twice we were treated to the wonders of the wavering ribbons of the Arora Borealis, the northern lights. With no electricity in those early years there was no ambient light—no yard lights or the glow on the horizon of some nearby city. It's hard to duplicate those experiences these days.

Bobby and Tommy at Moose Lake (Circa 1948)

On our own, Tom and I learned how to find the biggest night crawlers, catch and sell frogs, live-trap chipmunks that were stealing the chicken feed, and how to catch snakes out at the wood pile. Being the wise elder cousin, I taught my younger cousin Tom where the stinger is on a bumble bee, pointing it out with the tip of my index finger. He's never let me forget the lesson he learned.

Back in Minneapolis, Tom and I were often at each other's homes—taking the streetcar or riding our bikes from one place to the other. "He's here for dinner and the night," was a frequent telephone call between my mother and Claire or vice versa.

It's hard to believe, but when I was nine and Tom eight, we took the street car, an electric trolley, to downtown Minneapolis where we transferred to another trolley headed to the Minnesota State Fair in St. Paul. We were each given one dollar and a dime for the day. The dime was for the trolley ride home. Today's parents would be cited for neglect if they gave their children the freedom we took for granted. Tom and I went to the State Fair every year until we were in our teens, trading up over the years from the penny arcade and peepshows on the midway, to tractor rides on machinery hill, to the stadium to watch stock-car races.

After Claire's husband, Roy, died, Claire became part of the Taylor extended family, always present at every family gathering and celebration. Even well into her nineties, I knew Claire would be a rich source of family lore. She and Aunt Ann didn't always agree on events—Ann emphasized the storyline and Claire was a stickler for details—but together they wove a rich tapestry.

Back at the restaurant with Claire, I switched on the tape recorder. "Go ahead," I said.

"First," she said. "How's your mother?"

"Sue and I went to see her this morning," I said. "My sister Gail was there, too. Mom's not doing very well. She seemed happy to see us but I don't think she knew who we were, not even Gail. Gail says she gives herself points based on how much of a response she can get from Mom. One point if she eats something. Two points if she opens her eyes. Three points if she opens her eyes and looks at her. And four points if she opens her eyes, looks at her, and shows some sign of recognition. But Gail says she always responds to a pat or a hug. She'll lay her head up against Gail's hand."

"Gail says Hildur's afraid sometimes," Sue added. "She seems especially fearful of the men who come into her room. I can imagine. Some guy you don't know, some stranger, helping you with your bath. It's got to be scary. Even then, Gail says she always says thank you for whatever anybody does for her."

"Gail's good to her," Claire said. "She'll pick me up and take me over to the nursing home so I can visit. But it's hard for me. She doesn't know me either, and we were so close for so long."

Claire took a sip of coffee. "You wanted to talk about the cabin," she said. "There's a lot to tell, but what I remember most is the spring I got sick…"

15

A WALK THROUGH THE SNOW TO A ONE-ROOM SCHOOL

In early January, 1914, the morning school started after the holidays, there was an especially thick coating of frost on the rafters above Clara's head when she awoke. Glancing at the sparkling crystals, Vera and Clara each pulled an extra pair of wool stockings from the clothing basket to protect against what they knew would be a bitterly cold day. Hildur and Anna were too young yet to go to school with their older sisters. Even so, they arose and dressed before Clara could offer a prodding finger. If someone in the Back household slept in, it was because they were ill.

By the time they had finished breakfast the rising sun had brought light but little warmth to the forest outside the cabin. Through the trees the sky was pale blue, with no clouds to hold in what little heat the sun might generate during the day. About two or three inches of fresh snow had fallen during the night. The snow had come straight down with no wind to push it into drifts or to create depressions on the leeward side of trees and buildings. The yard was a soft, unbroken blanket of white cotton that undulated from the shallow hollow in front of the root cellar and rolled up over the rocks and stumps that lay hidden beneath.

After breakfast Vera and Clara sat on a bench inside the door pulling leggings on over their long stockings. They pulled on another pair of heavy stockings over their shoes. Neither girl had overshoes. Each girl had a small bundle to carry—a lunch her mother had prepared and a book (the reading assignment for the holiday break), both wrapped together in a cotton kerchief with its corners tied together in a large knot. After pulling on their coats and mittens, the girls picked up their bundles and walked to the door. Before stepping outside they looked expectantly toward their father.

Peter put on his coat and fur hat and took down his rifle and a single cartridge from a box on a high shelf. He pulled open the door and held it as the two girls preceded him out through the foyer. Outside, Clara turned her head and spit between her teeth. Her spittle froze solid in mid-air and hit the snow like a scatter of bee-bees. Vera gave Clara a stern look but their father just smiled. He checked over his two daughters to assure they were adequately clothed against the cold air. When it was this cold and the wind was blowing, any fool knew enough to cover up. But when the air was calm the cold could sneak up on you unless you were careful. You could freeze the end of your nose, or part of an ear, or a fingertip and not know until you came inside to thaw out. And then came the searing pain, as if the offended body part had been burned, yelling at you for your indiscretion.

Peter walked ahead of the girls, across the yard and out the pathway leading to the road. As he walked he shuffled his feet, treading a narrow furrow through the unbroken carpet. The girls followed his path, their feet crunching and squeaking through the snow. When they reached the road they all stopped and stood for a moment with their feet planted a few inches apart, looking and listening with intensity. There was no one on the road in either direction. There were no tracks of anyone or any creature having yet passed-by, either on foot or by sleigh. The road and surrounding forest were empty and undisturbed. No motion could be seen, not a sound could be heard. No wind, no other people, no trees creaking, no birds.

And no wolves.

"No wolves today, girls. With all this fresh snow they'll stay home until the deer start to move. No need to be concerned, but just in case." Peter drew the cartridge from his pocket, loaded the rifle, and fired a shot into the trunk of a large tree that stood next to the road. In the cold morning air the sharp report reverberated through the forest for what seemed like several seconds. When the echo faded the surrounding woods seemed even quieter than before, except for the soft plop, plop of snow falling from the high branches of the tree Peter had shot. "Off with you now," he said.

Peter was not overly concerned about wolves, nor were the girls. He had not heard about anyone being attacked by wolves anywhere in the area. But there *were* wolves around. At one time or another every member of the family had heard them howling. Once he had seen wolves on the road into Kelliher, two large gray-brown animals, their snouts red from feeding on a deer carcass. They had run off into the brush as he passed. But on his return later that day, he could see they had come back to finish their meal. He had never seen evidence of any wolves in the immediate area, no scat or paw-prints on his land or on his neighbor's land. Still, it was well to be cautious and a gunshot seem to give the girls confidence.

With a nod the two girls headed off down the road toward school. Vera, followed her father's example, led the way, shuffling her feet to make a path for Clara. Their father watched them for several minutes, their packages over their shoulders, their feet leaving an ever-longer trail in the snow. He smiled as he heard them signing, their sweet voices floating in the cold air.

The walk to school was a full two miles. The girls knew the route well. They walked it every school day, both ways. It was also the way they had gone for the Christmas pageant, only then it had been by horse and sled.

The walk took an hour, give or take, depending on the weather and the condition of the road. This morning the girls walked through the fresh snow with ease. The few inches that had fallen were light and the snow underneath was hard-packed and firm, holding their weight easily and allowing them to walk quickly.

"It's a beautiful day," said Vera, and Clara agreed. Like everyone in the family the two girls had learned to love the out-of-doors. What could be better? A walk in the woods, the ground covered in white, the sky an unbroken blue. Cold or not, it was a beautiful day.

When the girls arrived at school a couple of older boys were helping the teacher, Miss Olson, rearrange some of the children's desks.

Her sense of order had been disrupted, as well as the classroom furniture, for the Christmas pageant and she wanted things back in their places. Miss Olson addressed Vera as soon as she had settled. "Would you please wipe off the blackboard for us." It wasn't a request.

As the older children helped Miss Olson get things organized, Clara sat down on a long wooden bench and removed the stockings that covered her shoes. She brushed off the snow and hung them with her mittens on the drying rack that encircled the stove. She kept her coat on. One of the older boys had laid a good fire when he first arrived and the stove was already hot. But the school had been closed for more than a week and the building and all its contents were still ice-cold. Clara noticed that a pail of water, one brought in from the lake for the Christmas pageant, still sat on the floor by the blackboard next to where the tree had been, its contents now a bulging chunk of ice. On a day like today, even with a good fire, the stove would never do more than take the chill off the room. Except for the few who sat closest to the stove, most students kept their coats on. As Clara sat down at her desk she could feel the cold of the seat penetrate through her leggings. The desktop was equally frigid so she folded her hands in her lap and quietly waited for class to begin.

The classroom filled with students and the sounds they brought with them: the clomp of feet, squeals of greeting, laughter, the bang of desk seats being lowered, the squeak of shoes on the wooden floor, a general clamor of movement, noise, and voices. By now the drying rack was festooned with hats, scarves and mittens, the clinging snow slowly melting in the radiated heat.

Miss Olson stood at the front of the room and rapped a ruler against her desk. "Students!" she said in English. While all the students spoke Swedish at home, only English was allowed in the classroom. The students were immediately quiet. Miss Olson was a high school graduate, one of the few with that much education in the area. Only twenty years old, she had quickly learned how to control her students. She was just a couple of inches over five feet tall but sturdily built, with a no-nonsense demeanor. Her lesson plans were straight-forward and focused on three subjects—reading, writing, and arithmetic—the same for all her students, first through sixth grades, just more demanding assignments at each higher level. If her students were to learn much art, science or history, they had to do so somewhere else.

There was one eight-foot wide blackboard mounted low on the wall at the front of the room. The letters of the alphabet, both upper and lower case, were neatly scribed in cursive in white paint along its upper margin. Solid horizontal white lines had been painted on half of the blackboard, each line about four inches above the other. Halfway between the solid lines were lighter, dotted lines. When working at the blackboard a student was expected to write each letter carefully, replicating the cursive patterns scribed along the upper border. All letters were to rest comfortably on the bottom solid line. Capital letters were to rise to just below the upper solid line and lowercase letters to the dotted line. Tails that fell below the bottom line were not to go lower than the dotted line below. The rules were clear and everyone followed them, including Miss Olson.

Geography lessons, when they occurred, were covered by two pull-down maps hung on nails just above the blackboard, one of the United States and one of Europe. If students had a broader curiosity, a world globe stood on Miss Olson's desk. Next to the globe was a cigar box filled with an assorted array of chalk sticks, mostly white, each an inch or two long, with bevel-worn ends. On top of the chalk were two felt erasers, one of which Vera used to wipe the blackboard clean before class.

Miss Olson's students learned! Miss Olson knew these were children of immigrant parents who spoke little English. Most of her older students had not learned any English until they started school, but younger students, those with older sisters and brothers, were now coming to school better prepared. They were learning the language from their siblings, as were their parents. Students were required to speak only English, even among themselves. By the end of first grade every student could speak English, with a limited vocabulary but with no Swedish accent. By second grade they could read aloud and could write simple but well-structured sentences. By the end of fourth grade they all knew their multiplication tables, one through twelve. By the time they finished sixth grade every student could speak English in properly structured sentences, had a remarkably broad vocabulary, and could read a newspaper and most adult books aloud without stammering.

Class started promptly at nine o'clock. About ten thirty, after the morning lesson, students were allowed a fifteen-minute recess, a chance to go to the outhouse or spend a few minutes at play. Both activities required getting dressed for the out-of-doors. At the break, Vera and Clara eagerly pulled on their still damp shoes, stockings, and mittens and went outside. Both girls headed immediately to the large snowdrifts that blew in off the lake. The white mounds were near hollow in places, a web of interconnected tunnels and rooms, and remarkably strong because of the wind-packed snow. The two girls had been working together with a couple of their cousins to create a small room that would just seat all four of them. With a stick they were adding final touches to the interior, scraping the inner walls smooth, poking an air hole opposite the entrance to capture the breeze that always blew in off the lake. Excess snow was scooped out doggy style, between their legs, the one at the center pushing snow to one in the entryway who moved it on to another outside. Too soon they could hear Miss Olson ringing the school bell calling them back to class.

After school let out, Vera and Clara headed back home, retracing the path they had made earlier in the day. Except for their footsteps, the blanket of snow was still largely unbroken, most people and creatures of the forest had been smart enough to hunker in from the intense cold. At one point, though, they saw weasel tracks and then the ermine, in its royal white winter finery, standing on its haunches at the edge of the woods, its nose in the air, checking them out with its curious black eyes. And then, with a flip of its black-tipped tail, it was gone.

The sky was already beginning to fade by the time they returned to the cabin. As soon as they were inside and had pulled off their shoes and mittens, they warmed their hands and feet by the potbellied stove and were treated by their mother to a cup of hot chocolate and a cookie.

16

SPRING'S PROMISE BROKEN

Peter lifted a shovelful of wet snow. *It's as heavy as a bucket of water from the well*, he thought. He was especially eager to clear the snow from the entrances of the root cellar, the feed shed, and the outhouse. *If this wet snow freezes, the animals will starve and I'll need an axe to take a shit.*

Back in January frigid weather had continued for several weeks with daytime temperatures rarely rising above zero. February was warmer, if that's the right word, with daytime highs in the teens and twenties. By the end of the month everyone in the Back family was eager to see some sign of spring. When mid-March arrived, winter's worst seemed to be over. Temperatures moderated, occasionally rising above freezing for part of the day. The deep drifts along the edge of the hay meadow began to erode. Here and there brown patches of underbrush began to peak through the white blanket that had covered the forest floor for months. Lena and the girls had their hopes up, but Peter knew spring came reluctantly to the homestead, in fits and starts. Even if the trees began to bud out, the ice on Red Lake never broke up until late April.

Sure enough, late in March, all spring's progress seemed lost. A moist wind blew in from the southwest bringing driving snow with large, water-laden flakes. The wet snow attached itself to everything in its path. The south side of the cabin, the barn, the outhouse, and the bark of every exposed tree was plastered in white. Thin twigs not yet budded were turned to fingers of ice; tree limbs strained under the heavy burden of clinging snow. The branch of a large tree near the barn failed under the weight, snapped loose and crashed to the snow-covered earth with a muted thud, narrowly missing the building. Pine boughs drooped to the ground. Everything was buried again under eight inches of white.

But instead of freezing as Peter feared, the spring snowstorm was followed by a warm spell. The heavy snow began to melt quickly and water began to drip from every overhanging tree branch and run in haphazard directions. The land throughout the region was essentially flat and water pooled indiscriminately. Every pockmark was an invitation for a gathering of rivulets. Water stood in puddles and ponds, footpaths became streams, water began to rise in the well and the hole under the privy. Along the road the county's drainage ditches filled with water, but the water migrated slowly as if unsure where to find a still lower place on the earth's surface to settle. The roadway itself quickly cleared of snow and its surface began to thaw. At night the road's surface would freeze, but each day the hardpan would turn to ever deepening mud. It was already difficult to move through the muck with the sled and in another week it would be impossible by sled or wagon.

Vera and Clara's daily walk to school became a trial. Even though they made a game of trying, it was impossible to skirt all the water puddles and mud holes between home and school. By the time they took them off, their stockings and shoes were sodden and muddy. They had to sit through the school day with wet feet, the classroom only a bit warmer than during the coldest months. At recess and at the end of the day their shoes were still damp and the walk home lost its charm.

About a week after the thaw, Clara woke up complaining of a sore throat. Lena kept her home from school for several days and she seemed to get better. She returned to school the next Monday but by Thursday she was complaining again about her throat. Lena kept her home again for another week. One morning, about three weeks after she first complained of a sore throat, Clara was too tired to get out of bed. She had pains in her elbows and knees, her chest hurt, and she had trouble breathing. Lena and Peter were worried. Young children often died of illness. Every family they knew could talk about losing a child, their own or someone close to them. Now their little daughter was sick and they didn't know what to do for her.

"Inflammatory rheumatism," said the doctor. "Nothing to be done but keep her quiet for several weeks and hope for the best. She probably won't die, but she could end up with heart trouble when she's older."

Peter did not like this man. A couple of years earlier, when Lena was having trouble delivering Anna, Peter had ridden into Kelliher to get the doctor. He found him drunk and surly and he'd said, "Let the farm woman die," and had refused to come out from town to help. Thank God for Lena's sister, Katrina. She had reached in and turned the baby around and everything worked out fine, no thanks to this man. And now he was saying nothing could be done for Clara. "Just keep her in bed," was all he offered.

Peter had taken advantage of an April cold snap that firmed up the road. He'd ridden one of the horses into Kelliher to see the doctor and ask if he had any advice on what to do for Clara. After Peter explained Clara's symptoms, the doctor seemed to know right away what it was. He said she'd be weak for weeks, maybe months. She wasn't to strain herself in any way—strict bed rest. Peter thought the doctor's advice was probably okay and that's what they'd do. But he still didn't like the man.

When Peter got home that evening he told Lena what the doctor had said. Peter had already carried a mattress down from the loft and set it on a box frame near their bed. Clara had been resting there several days now and that's where she'd stay for weeks yet to come.

Lena sat on the edge of Clara's bed and watched her daughter sleep. She had slept a lot since she'd gotten sick. *From what the doctor says, I guess that's best,* she thought.

Clara was weak and hurting, small and vulnerable. Lena

remembered the time when Clara had been two and they thought they had lost her. The cabin had been crowded with visitors and as they began to depart Lena noticed that Clara was nowhere in sight. She'd been napping on her parent's bed and now she couldn't be found. Had she gone outside? Vera said she hadn't seen her. Had she wandered into the woods? Was she lost?

Peter and Lena started searching with the help of the few remaining guests. They searched around the house, in the outhouse, in the well. They looked in the barn and the feed shed. They were starting to search the surrounding woods when Clara emerged from the closet under the stairway, rubbing her eyes. The guests had disturbed her nap and she'd climbed into the closet where it was quiet and lay down on a blanket on the floor. Lena could still remember her worry and her relief. Clara had no idea the disturbance she'd caused.

Lena looked at her now. "Dear Clara," she whispered, "sweet, innocent Clara."

Clara stayed in bed throughout the spring. She slept in bed. She ate in bed. When she needed to go to the bathroom her arms and legs were so weak she could barely stand long enough to make the transition from bed to chamber pot. The aches in her small body were unrelenting, moving from joint to joint. First her elbows and knees hurt, then her wrists, then her ankles, then her elbows again. She had pains in her chest and she had no energy. She felt exhausted all the time.

It was late May before the pains began to subside and Clara began to feel a little stronger. Lena knew Clara was getting better when she started to complain about being bored. Lena and Peter took turns reading to her and Vera shared her school lessons with her. But it was June before her parents would allow her to be out of bed for more than a brief period. By then Clara was barely able to walk. Her muscles were weak and she moved about the caben from one handhold to another. She spent most of that summer just trying to gain strength.

By fall Clara had recovered enough to resume her household chores and to climb the stairs to the loft so she could sleep with her sisters. When school started, however, she was not strong enough to walk the two miles to school and back and her parents began to make other plans. For several weeks Vera brought Clara's lessons home from school and helped her with her reading and arithmetic assignments. In the meantime, Peter wrote to his mother, Christina, in Holmes City, and arranged to have Clara move there where she would be only a block from the school.

Hildur watched her mother weave Clara's hair into braids. Clara sat backwards on a chair, holding on to the backrest and wincing as her mother pulled first on one strand, then another, creating two tight ropes at the back of her head. Hildur thought her sister looked pretty with her hair that way. "Mommy, can I have braids, too?" she asked. But her hair had been cut short last summer and wasn't yet long enough.

Lena was preparing Clara for the trip to Holmes City where she would stay with her Grandmother Hjelm. Lena was sorry to send Clara away, but somehow Clara had to continue her schooling and it was just too hard for her to go to school here. In addition, Lena was seven months pregnant and knew it was going to be difficult to watch over Clara with a new baby in the house.

Clara was frightened and apprehensive. She didn't know Grandma Hjelm. She had been too young when she'd been in Holmes City to remember her at all. She knew Grandma Olson, she lived nearby, only a half-hour walk through the woods. She was nice enough and often put out prune pits in an empty matchbox. The nuts inside tasted like almonds, a special treat. And sometimes she had cookies. But Clara didn't want to live with her. Grandma Olson was old and didn't seem too interested in her or her sisters. One time, Clara remembered, she had been visiting Grandma Olson with Vera and Anna and Grandma had spent most of the time reading a book and hardly acknowledged the children. When it was time for the girls to leave, Grandma didn't even look up from her reading when each of the girls said goodbye. Clara, in frustration, had said, "Grandma, you're supposed to say, come back soon." Clara certainly didn't want to live with Grandma Olson or anybody else for that matter. She wanted to live at home.

Peter's mother agreed to take Clara. For the last four years, since her husband Hjelm-Pele died, Christina Hjelm had been running a small rooming house in Holmes City. She had plenty of room and the house was an easy one-block walk from the school. Grandma Hjelm had written that she would be glad to have Clara, for as long as necessary. And besides, Clara was old enough to earn her keep by helping around the hotel. "Send her down with Otto and John," she suggested, "when they come visit at Christmas."

On December 7, 1914, a few days after her eighth birthday, Clara left her family and her home in the woods. Lena packed a bag containing Clara's few clothes and a small rag doll that Lena's sister, Katrina, had given Clara when she'd been bed-ridden. Aunt Katrina had intended the doll for her own daughter but felt her niece needed something to occupy her time until she got well. Lena thought her sister had shown a great kindness. It was the only doll Clara had ever had.

As Lena finished Clara's hair she heard Peter's two brothers pull into the yard. They were taking Otto's sled, rigged with a grain box, into Kelliher where they'd catch the train to Holmes City. Peter would go into town with them and bring the sled back after dropping them off.

After stomping the snow off their feet, Otto and John Hjelm entered the cabin, still bundled in their heavy coats, their hats in their hands, their cheeks rosy from the morning ride on the open sled. With a brief hello to Peter and Lena, Otto went over to the stove and poured two cups of coffee and sat down at the table with the others. He handed one cup to John and then blew across the top of his own. "It's going to be a cold ride this morning," he said after taking a sip of coffee. "Wrap her up good."

"Yeah, yah got that right," said John, nodding and blowing across his own cup.

Peter lifted Clara into the sled's grain box and set her down on a bed of hay covered with a heavy wool blanket. He then wrapped her snugly with a second blanket. Over that he put another blanket. Clara peaked out from a narrow slit in her covers and up at the high sides of the grain box. She was warm enough but numb with fright. She would remember nothing of the sleigh ride into town or the long train ride from Kelliher to Bemidji and on to Alexandria.

When Otto and John, with Clara in tow, arrived in Alexandria they were met by their brother Manne Hjelm who had come to pick them up in his Maxwell. It was the first automobile Clara had ever seen. Clara was bundled into the back seat and wrapped again in blankets. While the car was enclosed with transparent curtains it was about as cold as the sleigh had been. By the time Clara arrived at her grandmother's home in Holmes City, about five miles away, she was chilled and feeling sick again. With barely a word, Grandma Hjelm put her straight to bed.

The next morning Clara slept until mid-morning and awoke with a runny nose but, blessedly, no sore throat. Clara was given a small room on the first floor, too small for a paying guest. It was the first time she had ever had a bedroom all her own. After breakfast, Grandma Hjelm helped Clara unpack her few things and put them away. When Grandma saw the doll Clara had brought she shook her head and said, "You're too old for dolls. You'll need to work."

Clara would stay in Holmes City for two years.

17

POOR IN NAME ONLY

"I stood on a chair next to the stove peering into a pot of simmering milk," I said. "My mother was stirring the milk with one hand and sifting flour through her fingers with the other."

"'This is how you make mush,' she told me."[16]

I was telling the story to my Aunt Claire, interviewing her once again, trying to fill in the blanks of my vast ignorance about life up at the Waskish cabin.

"It was one of my favorite breakfast treats—a gruel sprinkled with sugar and cinnamon and a dab of butter in the middle."

"We had mush all the time," Claire said. "Your grandmother would use the last of the milk, just before it spoiled. Sometimes she made foute-grout too, if we had some extra cream."

"We kids called it foot-grit when Mom made it," I offered. "So, you must have had a cow?" I asked. Nobody had ever mentioned animals at the homestead, and I was too ignorant to inquire, but it seemed obvious.

"Oh my, yes," Claire said. "We had a cow that my mother milked every evening, and an ox, Jim, and horses that Dad used to pull a sled in the winter and a wagon in the summer. They were kept in a small barn, right through the winter. We also had some chickens and every fall we butchered a pig. We had a big garden and there were lots of summer berries. My mother canned a lot, enough to see us through the winter. We were pretty self-sufficient out there in the woods."

"When I was a kid," I said, "Mom had a garden and she canned stuff every fall. There were shelves down the basement that were lined with preserved fruits and vegetables. Every now and then she'd send me down there to fetch a jar of this or that. Each jar had half an inch of paraffin wax on top. Some were sealed with a two-part metal lid. I liked to peel the rubber off the inner lid with my finger nail. If I was careful, I could peel it off in one piece, a rubbery ring like a rubber band but of no use to anybody."

"That was a victory garden," Claire said. "We all had one. It was part of the war effort. Everybody put up preserves."

"In the summer we had way too many radishes, if I remember right," I said. "But I was very fond of the slices of big ripe tomatoes sprinkled with sugar. I didn't learn until years later that nobody puts sugar on their tomatoes."

"Your mother learned that from your grandmother."

"Mom also kept an empty coffee can by the stove."

"Yes," Claire interjected. "That was for collecting grease and fat from cooking."

"What was that about?" I asked.

"They told us they wanted the fat to make bombs," Claire said.

"Really? I never knew that."

"Well," said Claire, "I think they also wanted us housewives to feel we were helping the war effort."

"When the can was full," I said, "Mom would tell me to take it to the butcher shop—they paid me a few pennies. Then I'd go next door to the bakery and buy a loaf of bread. I couldn't have been more than four or five at the time. Mom told me it took me forever to pick up a loaf of bread. She'd watch me coming up the street, strolling along, looking at the birds and squirrels or bending over to scrutinize some curiosity on the ground, the loaf of bread squeezed tightly under my arm. She said she had to pull those middle slices back in shape in order to make a decent sandwich."

"She told me that story more than once," Claire said. "She thought you were cute."

"I'm sure I was," I said. "When I was older, I asked her why she didn't tell me to stop squeezing the bread. She told me squeezed bread was a small price to pay for giving me the responsibility."

"And it got you out from under her feet," added Claire.

"That too," I said. "At some point she stopped with the garden. She kept some flowers, though. I remember tiger-lilies out back and little white-belled lilies-of-the-valley in the shade on the north side of the house. Every summer she planted red geraniums. But at some point we grassed over the vegetable garden, except for a tenacious clump or two of rhubarb. I'd pick a few stalks and Mom would make a tart-sweet sauce, one of my favorite desserts. But she quit the garden and quit canning. I wonder why?"

"It was too much work," Claire said. "And by then you were rich and there were good grocery stores."

Claire often referred to our family as the "rich relatives." I never thought of us as rich, but she did have a point. My dad had a good job at the University of Minnesota and we had a good-sized house in a nice south-Minneapolis neighborhood.

Claire paused, her eyes looking inward. "You know," she said, "we were poor on the homestead. We didn't know it at the time. All our neighbors were in the same boat."

She was echoing what I'd heard from Uncle Glenn and Aunt Ann.

"We never went hungry," she continued. "We had clean clothes. We had a roof over our heads and wood for the stove. But now, I look back, we were just getting by."

18

FRUITS OF THE FOREST

Peter was mending the picket and chicken-wire fence that surrounded the garden. The corner posts and pickets he fashioned himself from split cedar harvested from the property. The chicken-wire was an expensive luxury but one that had a two-fold benefit: it kept the pests out and kept his wife happy. But last night a rabbit had found a hole under the wire and had made a good meal of some of the young lettuce leaves. The rabbit now hung in the barn waiting to be cleaned but there were more of the long-eared pests out there. And there were deer that just loved the fresh sprouts of almost anything that grew. Peter had made the fence as high as his head to keep them from jumping in. He could feel their soulful eyes staring at him from the woods, waiting for any lapse, any opening.

And the cow, even the cow had no respect for boundaries. Given an opportunity, she would pillage the garden like a marauding Viking, horns and all. Earlier in the spring, Lena had found the cow stretching her neck into the woodshed's narrow door, just able to reach the flat of cabbage sprouts Lena had stored there for the night. Peter could not remember seeing Lena so angry. She planted more seeds, but even now the cabbages were a couple of weeks behind their garden-mates.

Lena had chosen her garden plot well—an expanse of flat earth near the house that was raised slightly above the surrounding terrain, just enough to drain the soil and keep the roots from drowning. When

Peter went fishing, he buried the remains here and there for fertilizer.

Peter surveyed the garden. In addition to rows of lettuce, spinach and cabbage; Lena had planted tomatoes and green peppers; rows of beets, carrots and onions; and mounds of cucumber and summer squash. Vines of peas and green beans climbed a wooden trellis. Knee-high stalks of sweet corn were lined up in formation along one fence line. A plot near the gate was devoted to basal, rosemary, parsley, mint, chives and other herbs that enlivened Lena's cooking. Another large section was devoted to row upon row of potatoes. Peter could not remember a dinner without potatoes.

Lena also knew where to look for June berries, plums, wild raspberries, small wild strawberries hiding in the low grass, and over on Bohlman Island bushes laden with blueberries. At harvest, Lena spent days preserving the garden's bounty in dozens of glass jars she'd stash in the root cellar for the winter.

Which reminded Peter to give the root cellar a once-over. It was only a few steps away from the cabin. It wasn't much of a cellar in that its floor was only a foot below ground level. If it were any deeper it might flood because of the high water table. Instead, Peter had built a square log frame above ground with a sturdy roof and a small door on one side. Inside, he lined the walls with shelves. Then he covered the frame and roof with a deep layer of clay soil and tamped it down. In the summer it looked like a grassy hillock and in the winter after a good snow, it looked like an igloo.

Peter checked the cellar for cracks and holes, especially around the door frame. He opened the door and stepped inside, stooping down to avoid hitting his head on the low ceiling. He had made the ceiling high enough for Lena but it was a little short for him. He checked the shelves. There were still jars of preserved vegetables and fruits, jellies and jams, and even a jar or two of preserved chicken and several bags of last summer's potatoes—plenty of food to last until the fall when Lena would again spend days harvesting and canning, restocking the larder for the long winter.

What Lena couldn't grow or pick, Peter could hunt. Game animals were abundant in the forests around Red Lake. Peter often saw white-tailed deer when he walked and worked in the woods and he could read their signs. He recognized individual animals by the tracks they left in the damp earth and he could tell how recently they had passed by and where they were headed. He could see their presence in the broken twigs of elderberry bushes and in the bark of low-hanging branches stripped bare from foraging. Matted grass and pine needles told him where they had bedded down for the night.

Rabbits could be found in the grassy meadows and walleye pike and crappies could be caught summer and winter from nearby Red Lake. Partridge (ruffed grouse) were generally plentiful, though for reasons Peter didn't understand, their numbers seemed to rise and fall from year to year. But even in a slim year, Peter knew where to look. In the winter he'd find them among the young aspen, feeding on the buds that formed in the fall. In the early spring he heard the cocks thumping, competing with other roosters for the attention of nearby hens. In the summer, as he walked a trail through an aspen grove, he was amused by the occasional head of a bird stretching up above the ground cover, curious about his presence and unmindful of its vulnerability. In the fall, after the foliage dropped, he might scare up a few birds and they would fly into a nearby bare-branched tree, confident they were out of danger's reach. Since he used a .22 rifle rather than a shotgun, he didn't try to shoot them in flight. He was hunting for his food, so an unmoving bird was a preferred target. Fortunately, partridge were dumb birds and particularly good eating. He never shot more than they could use.

In addition to game, a cow provided milk, cream, and butter for the household—and cottage cheese for the chickens. A dozen hens provided a ready supply of eggs, and a coop of growing chicks an occasional fried chicken dinner. Each fall Peter butchered a pig—making sausage, bacon and ham that he salted and then smoked in an old oil barrel. Other than feed-grain for the animals, the only items they regularly bought from the store were salt, lye to freshen the outhouse and soften the bath water, bluing for the laundry, and hundred-pound sacks of flour, oatmeal, chicken feed, and oats for the horses—each bag made of sturdy cotton, patterned with blue flowers, that Lena sewed into underwear, pajamas, and dresses for the girls.

19

PARTRIDGE IN A BARE TREE

As follow-up to our conversation at the family reunion, I called my Uncle Glenn on the telephone.

"Any luck finding that tape of Mom?" I asked.

"Not yet. I looked through some of the boxes in the garage but I haven't found it. I'll keep looking."

"I'm eager to hear it," I said. "I don't have any recordings of her voice. Let me know when you find it."

"I will. I haven't gone through everything," Glenn said, sounding a little miffed.

"Am I making a pest of myself?" I asked.

"No, no," he said. "I'm just frustrated I can't find it."

By now, I had interviewed each of my mother's siblings at least a couple of times and had accumulated a dozen or more mini cassettes—more than twenty hours of engaging conversations. I decided I needed to have the tapes transcribed so I could more easily reference specific events or pithy quotes. I took one of the cassettes to a transcription service and asked for a quote.

"If the others are like this one," the transcriptionist told me, "they will be difficult to transcribe and expensive. It's hard to recognize the voices and sometimes people talk over each other."

"Yeah, that sounds like my relatives alright," I said, and took the cassette back home.

I decided I would transcribe the tapes myself. It was daunting work with frequent pauses while my slow typing caught up with the dialogue and frequent replaying of sections to make sure I got it right. But I was entranced by their unique voices: the cadence and Minnesota lilt, their obvious warmth and fond reminiscences, and the richness of their storytelling. There was more there than I realized.

I was on a venture of discovery that kept me going for hours on end. I spent much more time making the transcripts than I did doing the interviews. The process drilled the stories into my brain. I also discovered gaps in my knowledge and compiled a list of questions I still needed to ask.

"So, Glenn," I said into the phone. "When we first talked, you said there was more to your dad's story than his being a good-natured lumberjack. Tell me more."

"I remember a time he took me out to the homestead," Glenn said. "It was a year or so before he died."

I could hear the catch in his voice before he continued.

"You know Dad died early, from pancreatic cancer. He was only sixty-seven."

"Yes," I said. "I was born a few months after he passed away."

"Anyway," Glenn continued. "It was the fall I started my sophomore year at Bemidji High School. We went out there to the homestead to cut firewood. We slept a couple of nights in an old tarpaper shack that was on our property. Late one afternoon, Dad wanted to visit an old friend who lived back in the woods. So he says to me, 'Maybe we can get a partridge or two on the way.'"

"We go down a logging trail, a deep ditch along one side. Most of the trees were bare. 'Well, look at that,' Dad says, pointing to five partridge sitting up in a tree. 'Do you think you can get one or two of those?'"

"Yeah, I say, and raise my gun, a .22 rifle, and aim at the top bird."

"'Oh, wait a minute,' he says. 'Don't shoot. Shoot the bottom one first.' So I shoot it and it falls to the ground. 'Do you think we can use more?' Dad asks."

"'Sure,' I say, so I shoot the bottom one on the ladder. It falls to the ground."

"Then he says, 'I don't think we need more than one more.'"

"'Yeah,' I say."

"'Well, then take the top one.'"

"So I shoot the top one and it falls down past the other two and they fly away. He knew what would happen if I'd shot the top one first. Dad would have said those birds were as dumb as county commissioners. It was one of his favorite expressions."

"As I said before, I never lived at the cabin. But my sisters told me an awful lot about what it was like. They were poor, by golly, but they were never hungry. Even so, it must have been a hard life. They had no money but somehow they got by. What with Mom's garden and Dad's hunting, they did okay."

20

ONE-SHOT PETE

Peter took his deer rifle down from the pegs above the cabin door. He racked the lever a couple of times to assure the chamber was clear then eased the hammer forward so it couldn't fire. He took a single cartridge from a box and slipped it into his coat pocket and stepped outside. He nearly always had a rifle near at hand—often a Marlin Model 1891 lever action .22 for birds and small game. But now he selected his Winchester Model 94 lever-action .30-30. It was the perfect gun for hunting in the woods—lightweight, easy to carry, and accurate at short range. He'd ordered the gun from a Sears catalog the first year they'd moved to the homestead. Lena got a Franklin treadle-action sewing machine and he got a rifle. They'd paid thirteen dollar for the gun and eighteen dollars for the sewing machine.

It was evening, a couple of hours before twilight faded, the end of a beautiful day in late summer. Earlier in the day, when he had been cutting firewood near Bohlman Island—a narrow hummock of land that rose from the bog on the east side of his property—he had noticed fresh signs of deer that liked to forage on the grasses that flourished there.

He walked off in that direction, following a dirt path that snaked through the boggy land, staying to the high ground and skirting the standing water. He was headed toward a big stump, the remnants of a huge Norway pine that had been cut down forty years earlier.

"Perfect," he whispered, as he settled himself on the edge of the six-foot-wide stump. From here he could spot any deer moving along the trail entering or leaving the island. He laid the rifle across his lap. He retrieved the single cartridge from his pocket and held it in his right hand. He calmed his breathing. He wanted to shoot a deer, but he wouldn't be too disappointed if all he gained from his effort was a quiet hour in the woods.

Peter was so consistently successful at hunting that he was nicknamed "One-Shot Pete" by a few of the neighbor men, although some thought the name might just as well indicate his success in fathering children. It wasn't that Peter was overly confident in his ability with a gun, although he was a skilled marksman, but he was exceedingly patient and cautious. He could sit for hours in one spot waiting for a deer to come along a trail or follow fresh tracks so quietly he could get a shot off before the deer knew he was there.

Peter acquired his caution as the result of a near calamity. One evening, the first year he'd moved to the homestead, Peter had been out hunting, hoping to shoot a deer to shore up the larder. He was sitting on this same stump, shielded by low bushes from a trail he knew was regularly frequented by deer. As he sat he saw the unmistakable flash of a white-tailed deer, flicking its tail as it fed in the underbrush. Peter quietly raised his gun to his shoulder. He took aim but was uncertain whether the deer's body was more to the right or to the left of its tail. As he was about to fire, a man walked out of the brush wiping his face with a white handkerchief. With a gasp, Peter quickly lowered his gun and sat back down on the stump, his heart racing. From that day forward he never loaded his gun nor aimed at anything until he was absolutely sure what he was seeing and he knew he had a clear shot.

Sitting quietly, Peter slowly raised his left hand and pinched a mosquito that was feasting on his neck. He brought the creature into his view and studied the smudge of blood between his thumb and forefinger. Just then, out of the corner of his eye he saw a deer, a two-year-old doe he guessed. Her head was up, her ears alert. She seemed to be looking right at him. He held his breath and sat perfectly still. At last she lowered her head and took a nibble of grass. While her head was down, Peter slid the cartridge into the chamber. He waited until the doe raised her head again, looked around and then went back to grazing. In one motion Peter lifted the rifle, cocked the lever, aimed and fired. The deer collapsed, its feet twitched, then lay still.

Peter approached the fallen deer with caution. He had seen mortally wounded animals kick their sharp hooves wildly, even jump to their feet and run off. He stood for a moment examining his prey, admiring its tawny fur and looking for any signs of life. He knelt down and placed his hand against the deer's neck, just below the jaw, feeling for a pulse. He closed his eyes and whispered, "Tack ska du ha," in appreciation for what the deer had sacrificed.

It took Peter an hour to drag the deer back to the cabin, hang it by its rear feet, slit its throat and drain its blood into a bucket. He eviscerated the animal and buried the innards fifty yards behind the barn. Before going to the cabin, he peed in a circle around the hanging deer to keep the night animals at bay. By the time he'd washed up, it was so dark the carcass was invisible from the house. He'd skin and quarter the animal in the morning.

"I heard the shot," said Lena, as Peter entered the cabin and hung the rifle back on its pegs. She assumed he'd been successful.

"I'll give a quarter to Mrs. Drothy," Peter said. "She's been having a hard time of late. There's still plenty for us and your mother and the Chellsons.

"I'm sure she can use it," Lena said as she went back to her sewing machine.

Like most of his neighbors, Peter didn't pay much attention to the constraints of the official hunting season. He harvested only what he needed and was generous with what he killed. The next day, after he had butchered the deer, he threw a forequarter over his shoulder and walked over to Mrs. Drothy's place, about an hour round trip.

A week later Peter got a letter, neatly typed, from the local game warden, a man Peter knew well. It said:

> *Dear Mr. Back:*
>
> *It has come to my attention that you recently shot a deer. While there is nothing I can do at present, you are surely aware that it is illegal to shoot deer out of season. Please refrain from this practice in the future.*
>
> *Sincerely,*
>
> *Elmer Johnson*
>
> *Game Warden*

A few days later, Peter learned from a neighbor that Mrs. Drothy had walked the three or four miles into Waskish to buy a few provisions at Mr. Miller's grocery store. While she was there Mr. Miller asked, "Well, Mrs. Drothy, I've got in some fresh meat. Could you use a little?"

Mrs. Drothy replied, "Thank you Mr. Miller. I appreciate the thought, but I've plenty of meat just now. Mr. Back was kind enough to share some of his venison with me."

In the lower corner of the letter, the game warden had scrawled a handwritten note, "Dear Pete: Be careful who you share your meat with."

21

ANOTHER MOUTH TO FEED

Peter walked into the cabin and saw Lena sitting on a chair, her teeth clinched and her face pale. It was a cold day in mid-January of 1915 and Peter had just finished a full day cutting timber. He was surprised to find Lena sitting down. She never just sat. She was always doing something—cooking, darning, sewing, or reading—something. And now, so close to supper?

"Get Katrina," Lena said. "Go now. I'll be alright with Vera until you get back."

Peter nodded his head, realization dawning—Lena was due any day. He turned around and went out to hitch a horse to the sled. Katrina was Lena's older sister and married to Pete Chellson. She had learned to be a midwife from her mother while they were still in Sweden and now attended most of the births in the area. She was good, too. She had a kindly nature and plenty of experience. She had been the one to turn baby Anna around when Lena was having trouble. That was when that damn fool doctor in Kelliher was drunk and had refused to come out to help with the delivery.

The Chellsons had settled near Upper Red Lake shortly after the Backs. They lived on the Tamarack River just south of Waskish, about four miles away. Peter figured he could be back in less than two-and-a-half hours. It was already getting dark when he set out. He lit the sled's oil lamp and threw on a couple of extra blankets for Katrina and was off.

It was a beautiful evening, the road straight and the snow well-packed. "Well now," Peter said to the night air, as he guided the horse through the rift of trees lining the road, "another mouth to feed. That will be five. I wonder if it will be a boy this time?"

When Peter arrived at the Chellson's, Katrina invited him to have a little dinner while she got her things together. She always kept a bag of essentials packed and ready to go and, anyway, she had expected this visit from Peter at any time. She was dressed in her coat, with bag in hand, in less than ten minutes. Peter took a last swallow of food, a sip of coffee, and followed Katrina out the door.

The ride back to the cabin was pleasant. The air was crisp with a canopy of stars spread across the firmament. He and Katrina were both dressed warmly; each with an extra blanket wrapped around their shoulders. Peter enjoyed Katrina's company. She was more talkative than Lena and always had a little gossip to share. He was impressed that her gossip was never critical of anyone. Much like Reverend Johnson, she could tell a good story or make a joke, and she always had a kindly word.

"Thanks for coming to pick me up, Peter," she said.

She thanks me? he thought. *I take her away from her family, at least until tomorrow, and she thanks me?*

"How are the girls?" Katrina quizzed Peter on the family, his work, what did he think about the article in the *Swedish American Post* about the war in Europe? Did he think America would stay out of the war? Did he know that Lena's oldest brother, Pete Olson, was saving to buy a car, maybe a Model T Ford? It would cost $850. It would take years to save that much, but it would make his job as mail carrier a lot easier.

Peter listened attentively and answered Kristin's questions as best he could. When there was a pause, he asked, "So, Katrina, will it be a boy or a girl?"

Katrina frowned. "You should have asked your sister-in-law, Sigrid. She'd know." Sigrid was married to Katrina and Lena's second oldest brother, Ole Olson. She had a reputation as a bit of a clairvoyant, although she denied it.

"Lena talked to Sigrid but she refused to make a prediction," Peter chuckled. "So, what's your guess?"

"You're pretty good at producing girls," Katrina offered. "I think you'll have another one."

"Another girl," Peter said. It wasn't a question.

"We'll know soon enough," said Katrina.

So, not a boy, Peter thought. He loved his four girls. They were healthy and well behaved. They had a scare with Clara, but she was well now and back in school down in Holmes City. The girls helped around the house as best they could. He had no regrets. Yes, a boy would be nice. But another girl would be nice too. *Either way, I'll be happy.*

Peter's apprehensions about a bigger family, another mouth to feed, were far outweighed by his pleasure of having another youngster around the house. He and Lena had not thought much about whether they wanted children. It was just what you did when you were married. It was considered a blessing, and Peter felt blessed. He liked children and Lena seemed to handle the birthing well, in spite of the trouble delivering Anna, and recovered quickly. And she seemed to handle the extra work that was required as well.

Peter knew that Lena wasn't so eager to take the children back into her lap once they were weaned. But she certainly watched over them and was kind to them. She just didn't show her love openly. Peter had always been the one that the kids climbed on. He had been the one to offer his lap, especially just before bedtime when he would sing to them or tell them stories.

It seemed only a few minutes and they were back at the cabin. Katrina took her things in as Peter settled the horse. He lingered a few minutes in the barn. He knew he would be mostly useless in the cabin. Katrina knew what to do and Vera would be a help. He reached in behind a can of kerosene resting on his work bench and pulled out a small bottle of aquavit. It was thick and syrupy from the cold and he took a hearty swig; the smell of caraway tickling his nose. He put the bottle back, out of sight. Peter didn't drink often but he found there were times when a little libation was needed. Lena didn't approve, just like she didn't approve of his occasional cigar or his dancing at parties. Still, she didn't give him a bad time about it. He thought he probably could keep the aquavit in the house, but he didn't want to go under her watchful scrutiny every time he wanted a swallow. Besides, he felt it wasn't good to drink in front of the girls. Fortified, the horse fed and settled, Peter blew out the lamp and walked back to the cabin.

Inside, Katrina already had the situation well in hand. Lena was on the bed behind the partition. Vera had brought in extra water from the well and had put on a large pot to boil. In a loud voice, speaking for Peter's benefit, Katrina said, "It won't be long. She's well along. Lena says read to the girls and get them ready for bed."

Which he did.

An hour later Peter sat looking at Vera who was curled up and asleep in her mother's chair. She was dressed for bed but wanted to be ready to help Katrina if needed. Peter had been trying to read the most recent issue of the *Swedish American Post,* but he wasn't making much progress. *I must have read that last paragraph three times*, he thought. He set the paper down and glanced up at the hole that led to the sleeping loft. He could see four small stockinged feet dangling over the edge of the first step. "Anna, Hildur," he said softly, "back in bed." The feet disappeared and he could hear the squeak in the rafters as the two girls climbed back under the blankets.

In another hour it was over. Katrina came from around the partition carrying a small bundle. "Meet your new daughter," she said.

"You're as good a predictor as Sigrid," he said to Katrina, then lifted the flap of towel that covered the baby's face. "Hello Selma," he said. "Welcome." Peter and Lena had already decided. If it was a girl, she would be named Selma Cecelia.

Now, five daughters, Peter thought. And that would probably be that. Peter knew Lena was happy to have another baby, but he thought she would probably say that was enough. Lena had turned thirty-five a month ago and now she has given birth to five healthy children. All girls.

Well, that's probably enough—for both of us.

22

THE EYES HAVE IT

Claire took a sip of coffee and set down her cup. "Did your mother ever tell you how she got poked in the eye?" she asked.

"Well, yes and no," I said. "She told me it happened, but she was never clear how. I remember she warned me about scissors. Don't run with scissors, she told me more times than I can count. And once, when I was four or five, I was cutting out some cardboard figures, maybe Red Rider or Tom Mix. I was using Mom's sewing scissors."

"She covered the scissors with her hand. 'Don't use those,' she said, and handed me a pair with rounded tips."

"But yours cut better," I protested.

"'Look at me,' she said, pointing to her left eye. 'See that little gray spot?'"

"I could see a faint discolored spot inside the brown iris that I had never noticed before."

"It was summer," Claire said, "the year before we moved to Montana. I was still living in Holmes City. Sally was just an infant. Ann told me that she and your mother were cutting pictures out of a catalog..."

23

BREAST MILK AND HORSEFLIES

Hildur awoke to the smell of mush cooking on the stove. She poked Anna. "Smell that?" she said. Vera was already downstairs helping her mother. Clara was still in Holmes City where she was living with Grandma Hjelm.

Hildur and Anna pulled on their clothes and climbed down the steep steps. The table was set for breakfast. As soon as Peter and the children were seated, Vera passed out bowls of steaming mush that her mother was filling at the stove. Each bowl had a dab of butter—a butter eye—pushed into a small indentation in its center, surrounded by a drizzled circle of maple syrup.

Peter sprinkled cinnamon on his mush and poured on thick cream. With his spoon he took up a bit of the hot porridge, making sure it had a little maple syrup on it, and dipped it in the butter eye. He brought the spoon up to his lips and blew gently across its surface before placing it in his mouth. "Umm!" he said, a look of satisfaction on his face. It was the only sound he or anyone else uttered until everyone had finished their porridge, each studiously following Peter's example.

The porridge was followed by scrambled eggs, fried potatoes, and thick strips of crisp bacon that Peter had smoked last fall. After breakfast, Peter left the cabin to do his chores while the girls cleared the table and washed the dishes.

While Lena sat in her rocker nursing Selma, Hildur and Anna

started paging through what was left of last year's Wards catalog. All the shoes and pretty dresses had already been clipped out of the tattered book, but that didn't diminish the girls' enthusiasm. Anna was wielding the scissors while Hildur looked on.

Anna looked over at her mother. "Mommy, did you know you can order a house from the catalog?"

"Ow!" cried Hildur, putting her hands over her face.

Somehow, Anna had poked Hildur in the eye with the scissors.

With Hildur crying and Anna screaming, "I'm sorry, I'm sorry," Lena got up from her chair and laid baby Selma in her crib. She took Hildur's face between her hands. "Here, let me see," she said firmly. "Take your hands away and look at me." Lena looked intently in both of Hildur's eyes. "I see," she said.

Without hesitation, Lena reached into her bodice, freed one milk-laden breast, and squirted milk into Hildur's eye. "It's just a scratch," she said. "I'll put a patch over it for a day or two. Don't rub it. Just keep your hands away. Here, wear these," she added, giving Hildur a pair of mittens.

Later, Lena told Peter about Hildur's injury. "It doesn't look too bad," she said. "I think she'll be okay but I'll keep an eye on her. If the eye looks worse, we may need to take her into the doctor."

They both knew that a trip into town, if even possible, would be an ordeal. It was late spring and the road into Kelliher was almost impassable. Peter's logging was done for the season—the road into town was no longer frozen and was now too muddy to haul a heavy load on the wagon without its wheels getting mired up to the hubs. If he needed to go to town, he'd ride one of the horses with Hildur in his lap. It would be slow, hard work for the horse, but if he needed to go, he'd lead the other horse as a pack animal, bringing back a few supplies.

For the next few days, Lena squirted a bit of breast milk into Hildur's eye, once in the morning and again at night. By the end of the week her eye looked fine. By the end of the month, the incident had been forgotten and summer was in full flower, the garden tilled and planted, the wildflowers in bloom, and the trees no longer dressed in their spring green. And with summer came inescapable hordes of vicious horseflies and evenings filled with the hum of swarming mosquitoes.

With the ground in the woods a little drier, Peter began the summer-long chore of cutting firewood. One warm morning in July, Peter picked up his axe and rifle and went out into the woods. He had rubbed a bit of mint in bacon grease on his neck and cheeks. He tied a scarf around his neck, pulled his wide-brimmed hat down around his ears, and stepped onto a dirt path that would take him some distance from the cabin. He immediately heard the buzz of swarming mosquitoes rising from the shrubbery. And with both hands occupied, he was helpless against their onslaught. The mint and scarf helped, but it would be a long, annoying hour in the forest.

After living several years on the homestead, Peter had already cut most of the standing deadwood close to the cabin. He walked until he came to a spot that had a few dead trees suitable to his purpose. He felled a couple and stripped their branches. He'd let them lie until he could come back with his saw, cut them into stove-cord length, and stack them to dry. He already had piles of drying firewood scattered throughout the property. In late summer he'd split and neatly stack the wood in the woodshed near the cabin and under the eaves along the cabin's exterior, one more insulating layer against the harsh winter cold.

By the time he finished, the day had grown hot. After lunch he asked the three older girls if they'd like to go swimming. Lena would stay home with baby Selma.

All three girls changed their clothes, putting on old dresses that Lena kept for rags—or make-shift swimming suits. Peter led them on the two-mile trek to the lake, singing an old Swedish folk song as they walked. The girls joined in as they skipped along the firm edge of the road.

The walked to the site of the school house where the shallow water stretched a hundred yards out into the lake. As they all wadded in, the water felt refreshingly cold on their legs, a pleasant break from the day's growing heat. A hundred feet out, the water now up to Hildur's waist, they paused. "Look at that view," Peter said. "You can't see the other shore. Maybe that's where the earth ends."

"Oh, Papa," said Anna. "It's just a lake. The world's round, just like the globe we have in the school."

"You sure?" asked Peter. "Looks flat to me."

Peter held Hildur's hands as she practiced kicking. The other girls dog-paddled about, splashing away.

"Ouch!" said Vera, and slapped her hand against the back of her neck. A large horsefly dropped to the water, its wings still buzzing.

"Ouch!" echoed Hildur, and slapped her arm. This time the horsefly flew a few feet away and circled back for another try.

"Quick!" said Peter, "sit down in the water."

They all did but Hildur popped up spitting water. "It's over my head!" she sputtered.

"Kneel then, said Vera, as they all splashed water over their faces to drive the horseflies away.

"Let's go home," said Peter. "Hildur, you lead the way, then Anna, then Vera. Stay close and swat the flies off the person in front of you."

The short parade sloshed its way to shore and marched for home, slapping and swatting the whole way. When they were safe inside the cabin, Hildur began to cry, but stopped when she saw her sisters giving her hard eyes.

"Change out of your wet clothes," said Lena. She glanced at Peter. "You too," she said.

As her family dressed, Lena heard the cow bellowing outside the kitchen window, her bell clanging loudly. Normally, the cow spent her day grazing on the grass over on Bohlman Island. Now, well before the time for milking, she was back, looking frantic, bawling, stomping her feet, shaking her head, and swishing her tail.

"Vera," Lena said, "please get the smudge pot from the barn." Peter had made one from an empty two-pound coffee can, adding a wire handle. "Smudge the barn first then bring it in here so we can do the cabin."

Half-an-hour later, Vera was back in the cabin climbing the steps to the loft, the smoking smudge pot in one hand. "It's like an oven up here!" she said. On a hot summer day, insufferable heat built up under the tarpaper roof.

"After you've smudged it good, pull the mosquito netting over the bed and open the screened window," her mother suggested. "Let a little air through."

That night, the girls climbed into bed and carefully tucked the mosquito net under the mattress ticking all around. They flopped on top of the bed covers dressed only in their underwear, hoping to catch even a hint of moving air.

Hildur swatted repeatedly at a surviving mosquito that buzzed near her ear. Then she heard one of her sisters make a sharp slap. "Got it!" Anna exclaimed with satisfaction. "I waited until it bit me."

Still, it was a couple more hours of sweltering misery before Hildur heard the rhythmic patter of raindrops on the roof. She sighed with relief as cool air from the window brushed against her skin. She closed her eyes, took a deep breath, and fell asleep.

24
THE DECISION

Holding his double-bladed axe in his right hand, Peter balanced an eighteen-inch long piece of cordwood in the center of the big stump he used as a chopping block. In one quick motion he swung the axe above his head and drove the blade into the end of the log, splitting it in two. He cut the two halves into quarters and threw the pieces unto the growing pile of stove-wood, then picked up the last log and repeated the process.

"Done," he said. "That's enough." He leaned on his axe and admired his work. The wood pile was now higher than his head and ten feet across at its base. It was the third like it he'd built over the last week. He needed to put up the coming winter's firewood before he left for Montana to work the harvest. By the time he returned in October winter would be knocking on the door. For a moment he caught his breath, thinking how he liked being here in these woods, savoring the satisfaction of a good day's work. He was doing what he wanted to do, exhilarated by the exertion and enchanted by the deep green colors and lush aromas of plants and trees in their full summer glory.

Still, Peter knew, their life in these woods was near an end. He and Lena had talked about it often. They agreed they could not make the homestead pay well enough to support the family. At current prices for timber, even if Peter was physically able to harvest every worthy tree on his property, it would only provide meager cash. And when the trees were gone, what then?

Peter's dream for the homestead had been modest, to be an independent lumberman, cutting and selling timber grown on his own land. He was confident in his abilities as a woodsman but the quality of the tree growth on their one-hundred-and-sixty-acres was too poor and the market price too low for the homestead to provide a decent living. Even if he cleared the land the soil was thin, mostly blue clay and poorly drained—just not suitable for crops. As Lena had correctly pointed out, if they couldn't make a living off the property as timberland and the land wasn't suitable as farmland even if it was cleared, how could they hope to sell it to anyone else?

And those county taxes! A year or two before Peter filed his homestead claim back in 1908, the county had started an ambitious project to drain the land around Red Lake. For eight years now, county engineers had been cutting deep drainage ditches and laying culvert pipe all along the roads that crisscrossed throughout the township. The authorities said they wanted to drain off the water so the land would be drier, more suitable for farming.

Peter knew the project was a bad idea. The land throughout the area was mostly flat and only a few feet above the surface of Red Lake. With the water table just below the surface, the water in the ditches had nowhere to go. What were they going to do, Peter wondered, drain Red Lake?

And the county was making him pay for the damn project! He and his neighbors were being assessed for the cost of excavating the ditches that bordered their properties. It was a dumb idea, and the deep ditches were a hazard to horse and sled. Here and there a large metal culvert lay on the shoulder of the road, waiting to be installed under a side road. Peter was sure county officials were getting a kickback, a commission, on the sale of each culvert. "There lies another county commissioner," he'd say as he passed one of the metal pipes, "sleeping on the job."

Peter wasn't the only settler to be disappointed with his free land. Many homesteaders across America had claimed land with high hopes but less skill than Peter. Even good land was difficult to farm when you had few tools and no experience. And not all the land made available for homesteading was suitable for farming. Some land, such as Peter's, was too dry or too wet or too rocky to be made productive. Even those homesteaders who had good land and who were experienced were often frustrated by draught, or flood, or high winds, or locusts, or claim jumpers, or hostile Indians forced from their traditional hunting grounds.

Compared to some other homesteaders, Peter got by. But the future of the Back homestead did not look more promising than the present. He just could not make it pay. For the last several years, in early August, he and a couple of Lena's brothers from Waskish had taken the train out to North Dakota, and more recently to northeastern Montana, to help with the annual harvest. The work was hard but the pay was good and helped to make ends meet.

Last fall, 1915, the year Selma was born and Hildur injured her eye, after Peter returned from the harvest, Lena and Peter had discussed the possibility of moving the family to Montana. Peter had made good money following the harvest. "It's so fertile," Peter told Lena. "Lush fields of big-headed wheat as far as the eye can see. The grain wagons overflow. Maybe we should try our luck out there."

Lena agreed and that winter Peter wrote his older brother, Andrew Nass, who had homesteaded near Westby, Montana, in the northeast corner of the state only a few miles from the borders with North Dakota and Canada. Peter asked Andrew to keep an eye open for an opportunity. Was there a place they could rent or buy into on terms? Peter urged his brother to talk it over with other members of the family who lived out there—Andrew's three grown sons, Peter, Jacob and Nels, who lived with him on his farm, and his daughter, Anna and her husband Bennett Nereson who had their own place. "Let me know if you find anything," Peter wrote.

That summer of 1916, as Peter was laying up firewood for the winter, Andrew wrote back. "There is a fellow I know, Ole Hellegaard, a Norwegian bachelor who has a good spread not far from here. He is going to enlist in the army and go fight in the war in Europe." America wasn't yet in the war, but the army was recruiting. "He wants to rent out his place for a couple of years while he's gone," Andrew continued. "Are you interested? If you are, let me know. You can meet him when you're out here for the harvest, look over the property, and work out the details."

Lena and Peter thought it might be just the kind of opportunity they were looking for. "We can rent for a couple of years, see how it goes, and maybe then claim a homestead of our own," offered Lena.

Peter wrote his brother. Yes, they were interested. He wanted to meet Mister Hellegaard in August.

Peter picked up his axe and drove the blade into the chopping block. He picked up an armload of the freshly split wood and walked to the woodshed where he dropped it to the ground. First, he took the remnants of last season's wood out of the woodshed and stacked it in rows next to the cabin. Then he started layering the fresh split wood into the shed, alternating the direction of each row to improve air circulation and give the stacks stability.

This may be the last time I do this, he thought. He sighed and brushed moisture from his cheek with the back of his hand. "I hate to give it up," he whispered, choking on the finality of his words. "This may be the end of this place."

25

MONTANA MEMORIES

"Do you remember this?" I asked Claire, as I pushed an old photograph across the table, a cracked and faded image in brown, sepia and yellow.

"Oh, yes!" Claire exclaimed. "That's us. That's our family. That's Vera, and Ann, and your mother in the front row. And Dad holding Sally, then me, and mother."

"Do you know when it was taken?"

"It was in Montana, the summer of 1918. We were at the Fellroth's, near Westby, for a picnic."

"You all look a little windblown."

Claire bit her lip and looked wistful. "Yes," she said. "It was always windy."

Windblown Back family in Montana (1918)

I showed her a second photograph of a group of sober-looking adults and ragtag children standing and sitting in the front yard of what looked like a farm house.

"That was also taken in Montana," she said. "It was taken the previous summer, in 1917. I was eleven at the time. We were all gathered at a neighbor's house for a picnic. It was right after the planting, I think."

"Do you recognize any of the people?" I asked. I had traced a copy of the photo, drawing a circle over each of the faces. I had already filled in a few names: Lena, Peter, Elvera, Claire, Ann, and Sally.

"Well, let's see," Claire said. "That's your mother. And this was Ole Hellegaard—we lived with him the years we were there. And this was Dad's brother, Andrew Nass and his wife Brita. And these were the Hendersons; it was their farm where the picture was taken. And here's Dad's sister, Ann Lundquist and her husband, Jonas from Canada. And in front are all my cousins and second cousins."

We spent ten minutes going over the photo. Claire would point out someone and I'd jot down their name in the appropriate circle. She was able to identify almost everyone.

"Who's this?" I asked, pointing to a boy sitting on the lawn near Claire.

"I didn't know him," she said. "He was just visiting. I never saw him again after that."

I jotted a note and slowly shook my head in awe. *It's been eighty years,* I thought. *What a memory!*

"Mom didn't talk much about Montana," I said. "She did tell me about the train ride across North Dakota, but that was about it. She must have been six at the time."

"Yes," Claire said. "That trip made a lasting impression on her."

"Tell me what you remember," I said.

"Well, it was hard," she began. "You know they had to pick me up in Holmes City on the way out. I had been living with my grandmother while I recovered from rheumatic fever. It was a long trip by train, and when we got there we lived in a sod house with a bachelor farmer. There wasn't room for all of us, so Elvera lived with another family where she cooked and cleaned. My mother cooked for the field hands. I helped her. We all worked hard."

26

WIDE-OPEN SPACES

The wheels of the wagon bounced and shimmied on the frozen roadway. Only a skim of snow and ice clung to the rutted surface, too little to use the sled. Peter stood at the front, his knees bent to absorb the jolts and shakes. The vibrations coming through his feet gave his voice an extra vibrato as he crooned an old Swedish melody. The horses' clopping hooves provided percussive accompaniment to his song, his breath pluming gossamer, white as a swan's wing against the deep blue sky. It was a crisp day in early December, 1916, and the Back family and all their possessions were on the bumpy road to Kelliher.

He's singing for the girls, thought Lena. *He can't be happy with this move, necessary as it is.*

But Lena was wrong. Peter was optimistic. He had seen the bumper crops, the grain wagons overflowing. Sure, it wasn't the forest, but they could make a good living out there.

Two heavy blankets had been laid over several inches of hay to help cushion the ride for Lena and the girls. Selma, now nearly two, sat in Lena's lap, the two of them wrapped in a heavy wool blanket. Vera, Anna and Hildur huddled under a second blanket, their faces exposed to the mid-day sun. Behind them most of the family's possessions were stacked and roped securely to the wagon's wooden bed. The dining table lay up-side-down—bundles of cook pots, dishes, and other kitchen utensils stitched tight in burlap and tied securely among its up-stretched legs. All the chairs from the cabin were tied together in a Gordian Knot of jutting arms, spindly legs, and rocking chair runners. Mattress ticking, emptied of hay, was stuffed with pillows, bed linens, and bundles of summer clothes, and now stitched closed, an ominous mass resembling a cheaply swagged casket. A couple of old canvas suitcases were set side by side, a loop of rope woven through their leather handles and tied down at both ends. Other burlap bundles were stacked here and there on the wagon, their contents shrouded in mystery until their destination: Montana.

Lena's brother, Pete Olson, sat with his legs dangling over the front of the wagon, a wool cap pulled down over his ears. After the wagon was unloaded in Kelliher, he would drive it back to his farm near Waskish. "Keep the horses and use them until I return," Peter Back had said. "Or, I'll write and tell you to sell them for me if we decide to stay."

In early October Peter had returned from Montana where he had worked the harvest. It was the second year he'd gone to Montana after several years following the crops in North Dakota. Again, he was excited by the bountiful harvest and feeling flush with the money he'd earned. And he had returned with exciting news: he had rented a farm outside Comertown, near Westby, from a fellow who was going into the army. "He's a bachelor," he told Lena, "living in a sod house. The house is big enough," he declared, "but pretty spare. We'll need to bring most of our things."

"We're moving to Montana," Peter had told the girls. "We'll take the train."

"Where's that," wondered Hildur.

"Not so far," said Vera assuringly, pointing out Montana's location on a map. But as she traced the route across Minnesota and North Dakota with her finger it looked farther than she thought.

When they arrived in Kelliher, the men unloaded the wagon and at the instructions of the yardmaster—a fellow Peter knew from the lumberyard—placed all their packages into the back corner of a boxcar that stood cold and empty on a sidetrack. "I'll keep an eye on your things until morning," the yardmaster said. "I hate to see you leave, Pete, but good luck to all of you."

The passenger fares and shipping costs were modest, a special bargain offered by the railroad to encourage folks to move out west. Lena had some extra cash—in addition to Peter's earnings—proceeds from selling the cow, the ox and several pigs. She knew that what they didn't spend for transportation they'd need to get started in their new home. Their possessions would be moved from boxcar to boxcar, following the family from train to train all the way to Montana.

After an overnight in Kelliher, the family rose before dawn and walked back to the train station. A little before six, Train #32, operated by the Minnesota & International Railway Company and bound for Bemidji, rumbled into the station.[17] Selma cried while Hildur and Ann stared in awe and covered their ears as the train's whistle blasted and smoke billowed and puffs of steam wheezed. It was the first train the children had ever seen, and even Vera, who was now an experienced traveler, stood in wonder. Lena and the girls clambered aboard while Peter assured that the boxcar with their baggage was hooked onto the train.

From Bemidji they took the Soo Line to Plummer and on to Alexandria and Holmes City where they picked up Clara, who was a little miffed to have been abandoned there for so long. Still, she was relieved to be done with the place and delighted to see her family again. Clara chucked Selma under the chin and said, "Hi, I'm your sister Clara. I'm pleased to meet you." She sized up her other sisters. She thought Vera looked more like a woman than a girl. "You've grown," she said to Hildur and Anna.

"So have you," said Anna.

In Alexandria they boarded the Great Northern to Minot, and then onward via the Soo Line across the endless fetch of North Dakota.

Hildur, six years old, sat with her elbows on the windowsill as the train rumbled across North Dakota. Golden grass, tinged with reds and browns, blanketed gently rolling fields stretching to the horizon. The landscape was so open and distant, so different from the forest on the homestead that surrounded her, covered her, held her close. Here the countryside did not change much from mile to mile—long stretches of open ground, the sky extending out as far as the land, so few landmarks to guide your way, a place easy to get lost in. The train seemed to float above the ground, gently rocking back and forth. Mile after mile, if it had not been for the telegraph poles that rushed by the window and the clatter of the train's wheels on the iron rails, it would be hard to tell if they were moving at all. Now and then they crossed over a dry creek bed with leafless bushes clinging to its banks. Occasionally she saw a tuft of bare trees sprouting from a crease in the undulating landscape, something to catch the eye, to give anchor. As the afternoon wore on the scene remained repetitive and monotonous. The sun began to fade and Hildur's eyelids drooped. Her head fell against Vera's arm as she dozed, the last of the Back family to succumb to the train's hypnotic motion and the landscape's unrelenting sameness.

Huffing and squeaking, their train had pulled out of Minot in the early afternoon, stopping briefly in several small towns—Coulee, Powers Lake, Appam, and Hanks—to drop off mail and an occasional passenger. When Peter had taken this same train back in August it had been filled with itinerant workers headed for the harvest, men dressed in bib overalls and heavy shoes, threadbare coats and sweat-stained felt hats pulled down close to their ears. On this trip, at each little town, few people got on or off. There was no need to deliver wheat or oats to these towns, they grew enough of their own and ground their own flour. But they did need coffee, sugar, lantern oil, paint, tools, bolts of cloth—and lumber, there were so few trees in the area. Hundreds of items were sent by rail from the larger cities back east to stock the inventories of small-town merchants and for farm wives eagerly awaiting packages ordered from Savage and Sears Roebuck catalogs.

At each stop the Back family waited while goods were unloaded onto the station platform. In Powers Lake they watched while a whole boxcar of merchandise was uncoupled from the train and left on a siding. But they didn't wait long anywhere. The train crews knew just what to do at each stop with no wasted motion.

It was dusk when they pulled into Westby and Peter knew they were now in Montana. Comertown was the next stop. At 6:45 PM, on a cold day in December, 1916, Peter and Lena Back and their five daughters arrived in Comertown, Montana, on time and in the dark.[18]

Montana seemed to hold so much promise. The earliest Montana settlers had gravitated to the west and central sections of the state with their cattle-friendly grasslands and abundant water for crop irrigation. The drier northeast corner of the state near Westby and Comertown lagged behind until the early 1900s.

When it was established in 1909, Westby was the most westerly town in North Dakota but was soon moved across the border to become the most easterly town in Montana. In an exercise of restraint and civic pride, the city fathers did not change the name to Eastby. One incentive to be in Montana was that the state, unlike North Dakota, didn't have prohibition. Coincidently, all Westby's saloons were already located on the western side of the border.[19]

As an incentive to settle the region, the homestead laws were liberalized in 1908 to double the amount of land that could be claimed, from 160 to 320 acres, and reduce the years needed to prove one's claim from five to three.

The Soo Line, eager to expand its markets westward, initiated rail service to Westby in 1914 and promoted the area's bounty, targeting immigrants from Scandinavia and Germany. The railroad's optimistic assertions were reinforced by the abundant yields and the high price of grain driven up by the war in Europe. Homesteaders flocked to the area, included several of Peter Back's relatives. With the influx of settlers, Westby, Comertown, and the whole northeastern region of Montana, boomed.[20]

Peter had seen the land's bounty for himself. On his annual pilgrimage to work the harvest in the area, he had been stunned by the overwhelming abundance of grain that spewed out of the threshers and spilled over the sides of the huge grain wagons. He had been awed by the new, gigantic, steam-driven farm equipment that made it possible to plow, plant, and harvest the sod-bound lands that dominated the area. And he and Lena had been impressed and grateful for the money he earned.

It was all exciting and promising and Peter and Lena wanted to be part of it.

27

SODBUSTERS

They stayed the night in Comertown's boarding house, a few steps away from the train station and nearly vacant, the harvest workers long gone. They had telegraphed ahead and, as agreed, mid-morning the next day Ole Hellegaard arrived in town with a horse and wagon to pick them up. In less than an hour the Backs and all their possessions were loaded and on their way to their new home. Lena and the girls found the best seats they could among the packages in the back. Vera made sure everyone was well covered with blankets. Peter, with the flaps of his fur hat tied down to protect his ears from the biting cold wind blowing in from the west, sat on the bench-seat next to Ole.

They headed east out of Comertown for about a mile, then turned due north toward Hellegaard's place. They passed through a trace of bare-branched cottonwood trees that followed a dry creek bed, then slowly climbed a long rise to the crest of a hill. "Look there," Ole said as he swept his arm in a wide arc. "That's my favorite view."

Lena and the girls stared open-mouthed across miles of dry grassland toward the distant horizon. The narrow dirt road ribboned into the distance, twin wheel tracks rising and falling over the gently rolling landscape. The whole scene was canopied by an endless overcast sky giving way to patches of pale blue and a low-hanging heatless sun. Except for the squeak of wagon wheels and the clop of the horse, the ride was quiet.

For the first few miles Lena and the girls were too busy gaping at the landscape to say much. It was all so new, so different. The girls were curious but disoriented and a bit apprehensive. Lena thought it was one thing to be an observer, watching the scenery go by on the train, but quite another to be immersed in it, to be part of it. The land seems so much more expansive, so unending. There were few edges, no way to mark this place from that place. The roadway here was nearly indistinguishable from the fields, just lines tracing through the rolling hills of dry grass.

As they continued their ride, Lena started to notice details and slowly adjusted her earlier impressions. Yes, there are edges, she decided, where the harvested fields have been plowed, all straight lines, parallel furrows rising and falling in lock step over the undulating earth, stretching out forever. At the bottom of a hill they passed through another dry creek bed and a clump of trees—cottonwoods she thought, bare-limbed and forbidding.

Then a farm, a sod house, with a door and one window, built on a hilltop and looking much like the hill itself. There was a barn made of rough-cut lumber and a windmill surrounded by a high fence and a corral with horses drinking from a wooden trough. A large odd-looking wheeled wagon, one side much higher than the other (to deflect grain spewing from the threshing machine she was to learn), stood next to the barn alongside another wagon like the one they were riding in. Further on they passed another farm, this one with a square wooden house standing on a treeless rise. Lena thought it looked forlorn, not firmly attached to the ground and somehow out of place. Next to a small barn stood a huge machine with a smokestack like a railroad locomotive and metal wheels larger than a man. A steam-driven tractor, Lena thought. What a beast!

In less than two hours out of Comertown, the wagon pulled off the road just past a small stand of cottonwoods and Ole announced, "Here we are." He reined in the horse and stepped down from the hard wooden bench.[21]

Peter followed. "Wake up, we're home," he said, as he slapped his numb backside and the children giggled. The two men helped the others shed their blankets and climb from the wagon.

Lena had been forewarned, but she had never seen a sod house up close. The structure was a little wider than their Minnesota cabin and half again as long. There was a wooden door and one window on the south side and another window on the west side looking to the trees and the road just beyond. *What's this going to be like?* she wondered.

North of the house stood a windmill next to a barn and a corral enclosing a few horses, a pair of oxen, and several cows. Next to the house was a small hillock with a door, the root cellar no doubt. Behind the sod house, Lena could see the corner of an outhouse. *Well at least the barn and privy are downwind and not in the front yard,* she thought.

Now face to face, Lena noticed that Ole had a several-day-old growth of beard and a couple of buttons missing from his flannel shirt. A bachelor, she thought, with no woman in his life, and a peculiar Norwegian accent. *He'll take a little getting used to.*

Lena stood for a moment and studied the cabin. Its ragged sod walls were thicker than her arm was long and slanted inward from the base up toward the roof line. The windows were small, maybe a couple of feet square. *That wood house we passed looked forlorn,* she thought, *but it was a proper house.*

Ole could see Lena's concern on her face. "I built it myself with the help of a couple of neighbors," he said. "The doors and windows and tarpaper for the roof came in by rail and I cut the sod right where she stands."

Lena scanned the area surrounding the cabin: for thirty feet in every direction the ground had been stripped bare of sod, just trampled earth.

Ole walked over to the cabin and laid his hand against the wall, his splayed fingers spanning a single layer of sod. "You can see, the sod around here is thick and tight. We laid each piece grass-side-down." He stepped back and raised his voice so everyone could hear. "The place is simple but it's comfortable, cool in the summer and warm in the winter."

Lena nodded her head in acknowledgement. *The place won't blow away,* she thought, *but I wonder what it's like when it rains?*

The children didn't say a word but Clara wrinkled her nose and Hildur followed her example.

"Come in and have a cup of coffee," Ole said. He entered the cabin first, stoked the coal fire in the stove and put on a pot to heat. "We'll have coffee in a minute," he promised.

As Lena stepped into the cabin her first thought was, *It's so small.* From outside the place looked bigger, but inside, the thick sod walls seemed to squeeze inward. That thought was followed closely by, *It has a dirt floor! How do I keep a place like this clean?*

The house was all one room with a curtain divider between the kitchen and the main part of the cabin—and no sleeping loft. In the kitchen there was a cook stove, *adequate*, she thought, and a sink under a deep set window with a bucket underneath and a shelf above. There was no table but a long wide shelf along one wall about four feet off the floor. A haphazard array of items—cans of food, jars of coffee and sugar, a cast iron skillet, a stack of mismatched dishes and cups, a wooden spoon and a metal spatula—were spread along its length. Beyond the curtain there was one chair and a low bed in one corner, and nothing else. The place was spare and surprisingly orderly but, to Lena's observant eye, dirty.

A bachelor for sure, Lena thought.

Ole took cups from the long shelf and poured coffee for Lena and Peter. The coffee was hot and bitter, often reheated and too long on the stove. Ole offered the children cookies. *Where did he get those?* Lena wondered.

They stood around in the kitchen, drinking coffee and nibbling cookies, while Ole told them his story. "I've been rejected by the army," he said. "I've got one bad eye and they won't take me. I'll honor our agreement though. The place is yours. But I'll stay on and work as your hired hand. I'll sleep in the kitchen." His declaration came out in a rush.

Peter and Lena looked at each other. *This is a surprise*, Lena thought. *I bet he hasn't said that much in a month.* Lena gave a slight shrug and surveyed the cabin's interior. *We can't all fit in here, even if he does sleep in the kitchen.*

As Lena struggled with her disquieting thoughts, she heard another wagon pull into the yard. It was Andrew Nass, Peter's brother, and his wife, Brita, and their son, Nels. They had driven over from their homestead north of Westby, about a three hour buggy ride. "We've come to help you get settled," Brita said as she stepped down from the wagon. "And we've brought lunch."

Inside, Lena and Brita looked around the room. Lena placed her hands on her hips and asked, "How can we all fit in here?"

"Andrew says there's a family near us that wants someone to help out around the house," said Brita. "Maybe Elvera would want the job."

Vera looked stricken but didn't say a word.

"I had hoped we'd all be together for a change," Lena said, then nodded her head in resignation. "Let's get this place straightened up before we unpack our things. Vera, Clara, give us a hand."

Without a word, Brita took a pail from under the sink and handed it to Peter. Peter placed his hand on Ole's shoulder and guided him toward the door. "Show me the well, Ole," he said.

Lena took a dishtowel and wrapped it around the head of a broom she found behind the door and handed to Vera. Vera took the broom to the far end of the room and stood there looking with dismay at the sod walls. "It's all just dirt," she said.

Brita walked over and stood next to Vera. "Be gentle," she instructed. "Just try to get the spider webs off the ceiling. You can knock off the loose chunks of dirt on the walls, but be careful." As Vera began her work, Brita talked to Lena. "I know a woman who lives in a house like this. She whitewashed the walls and covered the ceiling with muslin to catch the bits of sand and dirt that sprinkle down from time to time. I've brought a couple of extra bedsheets if you want to use them."

After working part way around the room, Vera walked over to the door and stepped outside. She took a few strides away from the building and shook the broom vigorously, the accumulated dirt drifting off on the breeze. She left the cobwebs on; she knew their stickiness helped hold the dust. Then she went back inside and returned to her cleaning.

Back from the well, Peter placed the pail of water on the stove, shook a few pieces of coal from the scuttle into the fire box, and stoked the fire. Peter had noticed that Ole had a good supply of coal in a large bin outside, dug into the cabin's earthen wall, with a door through to the interior where the coal could be shoveled into a small, covered coalbin. *This will be different*, Peter thought. He was used to a wood-burning stove but knew that timber around here was too precious to be used for fuel.

The women worked the rest of the morning—dusting every ledge, crack, and shelf, wiping the dusted areas with a damp rag. Lena scoured the enamel sink and the surfaces of the stove that weren't too hot. The dirt floor was firmly packed so she gently swept the edges and corners where small clumps of unknown origin had accumulated. Lena thought some of the small clumps looked suspiciously like mouse droppings. She shook her head but didn't say a word. *Well, I had some of those back in Minnesota,* she thought.

At noon, Brita unpacked a large lunch basket.

"Bless your heart," Lena said.

After lunch, Peter turned to Andrew and Nels. "Let's unload your wagon so you can get back home." Brita had brought a winter's supply of preserves—a collection of contributions from several of her neighbors, plus her own—which she helped Lena stow away in the root cellar. She also brought some staples that she knew Lena would need for cooking. Andrew and Nels unloaded bags of flour and oatmeal.

When the wagon was empty, Peter hugged his brother and whispered, "Thank you."

Lena put her hands on Brita's shoulder and said, "I can't thank you enough."

Brita said, "You're welcome." She looked at the sun low in the southern sky angling to the west. "I wish we could stay to help more but we need to start back."

After their goodbyes, Lena looked around and said, "Okay, we can start. Bring in the table first." Peter and Ole had already untied the bundles from among the table's legs. They wormed the table through the cabin doorway and set it down in the kitchen. "It won't fit there," said Lena. "Not with the bed in here. Put the bed on the other side of the curtain," relegating Ole to the back corner of the house.

Ole didn't say a word. It was his house, but he recognized the voice of authority when he heard it.

Next came the bed platforms and then the chairs, one by one, the Gordian Knot broken. Vera undid the stitches from a bundle of pots and pans and pulled off the burlap. Peter was given the mattress ticking. "You and Ole go to the barn and stuff these with hay," Lena instructed.

When the two men returned they pushed Ole's bed frame up against the back wall where Lena thought it wouldn't be too much in the way. Ole's mattress was brought in from outside where Clara had beaten it with a broom and laid it out to freshen in the sun. They set up two beds in the main room, one for Lena, Peter and young Selma, and one for the older girls. Peter and Ole rehung the curtain so it separated Ole's space from the rest of the house. Peter's and Lena's rocking chairs were backed up against the curtain, with a small table in between. Ole's chair was placed on the other side of the curtain facing his bed.

Lena wanted to hang the clothes on nails above each bed. Peter stood looking at the wall. "How do I do that?" he muttered. Clothes were laid out on the beds awaiting a solution.

"You can drive stakes into the walls," Ole suggested. "They'll hold pretty well. I've got a few out in the barn we can use. And we can string a couple of ropes, if need be."

Dishes went into the cabinet they had brought from Minnesota. Cooking pots and utensils, along with staples and canned goods, were placed on the long shelf in the kitchen, with bins for flour and oatmeal tucked underneath. Following Lena's instructions, Peter hammered in more stakes: hooks to hang his gun, the broom, Lena's aprons, more kitchen pots. Lena wanted everything off the floor.

Everything unpacked and in its place, Lena eyed Brita's muslin and the piles of burlap, now empty and unused. "Peter," she said, "can we hang the bigger pieces on the back wall? Use the sheets Brita brought. We can use the burlap to cover the other walls."

The day was fading when Hildur ran in from outside. "Daddy, Mommy, come look! Come see the pretty sunset."

They all followed Hildur out to the yard, wrapped in their coats and hats, their hands deep in their pockets against the evening's chilly wind. Hildur stretched her arms and twirled in a circle. "See!" She squealed.

High clouds, thin ribbons of pastel pink, floated above their heads in every direction.

Peter and Lena slowly turned to take in the view. To the south, fields of dry grass stretched outward and up a far rise to the crest of a low hill, maybe a mile away. To the east, their eyes followed the gentle rise of another hill, its crown glowing with the golden light from the setting sun. To the north the fan on the windmill and the roof of the barn were a rosy pink, while the barn itself was already in shadow.

When they turned back toward the west, Lena gasped. "The trees!" she said. "I hadn't noticed the trees." Half a dozen cottonwoods traced a thin line along the road, their bare branches in stark relief against the amber-colored hill that rose beyond.

"There's a natural spring in there," Ole said. "It comes right up out of the ground. We've got a pump, too. Good drinking water, and for cooking, and cold for keeping the milk fresh. The windmill fills a tank—for the livestock."

Lena was still staring at the trees. *How could I miss them?* She thought. She also noticed that their new home sat in the bottom of a broad shallow bowl of land. The land rose in all directions. Stark, yes, with little color except in the expansive sky. But the land was not as un-ending as she first thought and she was comforted by the familiarity of the trees.

Peter had seen skies like this before, but Lena and the girls were awed. The color wasn't just overhead as it had been back in Minnesota's woods. Instead, in every direction there was a vast painted canopy suspended above rolling fields of grain stubble, plowed earth and amber grasslands.

"It's beautiful, isn't it?" said Ole.

"Yes," acknowledged Lena, "but a bit overwhelming, too."

"You'll learn to love it," Ole said.

Maybe he's right, Lena thought. *I have to give it a chance.*

Peter looked at the high thin clouds. *There's a change in the weather coming*, he thought.

Shortly after sunset they quit their work and Lena and Vera started preparing supper—drawing from the remnants of Brita's picnic lunch and the foods Lena had found around the cabin. She had more to draw on than she expected. They had a sizable root cellar filled with several bushels of potatoes, carrots and other root vegetables. And thanks to Brita, there was also a generous array of canning jars filled with preserved green beans and beets. Ole said he didn't know all that was out there, but Brita had brought over a lot of things. Lena had brought some of her own preserves from Minnesota, plus a few bushels of potatoes. She was pleased to see what was already in store. Again, she thought, *Brita, bless you.*

"You can put the leftovers in the window, there," Ole said after dinner, pointing to the window opposite the door and away from the heating stove. The window was set two-feet deep in the sod wall, with a canvas curtain that could be drawn across the opening. "It's as good as an ice box."

"Good," said Lena, nodding her head.

Tired from their long days of travel and work and satisfied after a surprisingly fine meal, they were ready for bed. Ole was already asleep in his space beyond the curtain, snoring loudly. Lena grimaced. "That's going to take some getting used to," she whispered to Peter.

Little Selma was already asleep in the bed where Peter and Lena would join her shortly. Vera, Clara, Anna and Hildur all climbed into the other bed, two at each end. It was one of the few times during their years in Montana that the entire Back family slept under one roof.

Peter and Lena were exhausted from a long day but satisfied with all they had accomplished. They were settled in their new home and beginning life in a new land filled with promise. As the night wind began a low moan, masking the drone of Ole's snoring, their hopes were high.

But their timing could not have been worse.

28

HARSH AND BRUTAL LAND

It was a cold night in January, 1917, and Peter lay on his back listening to the wavering pitch of the wind's whistle as it swirled and eddied around the sod cabin. Out on these open plains there was always a wind, both summer and winter. Even with the trees to the west, most nights the wind hummed with a low moan. But tonight Peter had been awakened by a sudden change in the sound. He hadn't noticed the wind's noise when he went to bed. It had no doubt been there, as it always was, but he had ceased to hear it. It was like the summer crickets back home, unnoticed in their constancy, brought to consciousness only if they stopped. But the wind hadn't stopped. It was so much more intense, a devilish choir of inharmonious screeches.

It was their first winter in Montana and snow had arrived with a vengeance. There had been a dusting of snow a few days after they moved in and then a moderate storm around Christmas. Peter had been skeptical of the stories he had heard from Ole and his brother—raging blizzards, snowdrifts covering the house, cattle frozen where they stood, their nostrils clogged by the ice of their own breath. But as he listened to the wind, he was coming to believe that maybe their stories had not been exaggerated. "We don't hold school from December through February," Andrew had said. "It gets too dangerous for the kids to be out."

Peter knew Montana winters were not like they were back in northern Minnesota. Back there it was cold, but here the wind made it seem even colder, cutting its way through the seams of his clothing, pushing the chill through his skin into his bones. We had snow back there, Peter thought, lots of snow. It blanketed everything. Mostly it came quietly. Sometimes it was pushed by the wind, but the all-surrounding forest broke up the worst of it. Here, those few bare trees to the west barely stood in the wind's way. Here the wind was like a herd of buffalo that once roamed these lands, chased by a band of arrow-shooting Indians, cresting the hill off to the west and snorting its fear and furry as the mass of animals stampeded into the valley. *If the snow got in front of that wind...*Peter shivered.

After breakfast Peter stood at the window over the sink, helping Lena dry dishes and staring out at a vanished landscape. There were no visual clues beyond the glass. No hills, no barn, no root cellar door, no horizon. All was blank. It wasn't even clear that it was snowing, but Peter knew it must be! There was light, but it was diffuse, with no shadows. *So many snowflakes rushing by the window,* Peter thought, *but they're not visible. Just white!*

Ole Hellegaard seemed unconcerned. He had seen it like this more than once. The previous winter, the winter of 1915-16 had been brutal—the worst anyone could remember. This last December, Ole had insisted that he and Peter string a long rope from the cabin door to the barn, and another to the root cellar, and a third to the privy. They tied the ropes up on fence posts, each about four feet high, the ropes hanging between in draping loops. "When we get a blizzard," Ole had told Peter, "the wind comes out of the north, out of Canada. You leave the house and hold on to that rope for your life. You let go and you may never find your way back."

Peter had been skeptical, but he had noticed that many of the farms along the road had also strung ropes. Now, looking out at nothing when he knew he should see something, he was becoming a believer.

The storm continued through the whole day, throughout the night and into the next afternoon with the wind howling incessantly. The view through the window never changed except to go from white to black to white again. Going to the barn to tend the animals, not once but several times, had been an experience Peter would never forget.

After breakfast, with the unnecessary urging from Ole, Peter bundled up against the wind and snow, the earflaps of his cat-skin hat tied securely under his chin, his hands protected with gloves and mittens. The two men set out toward the barn, Ole leading the way, each man leaning into the wind, one hand sliding along the security rope. Except for the feel of it in his hand, Peter thought it was almost impossible to tell if there was a rope there at all. He could see only a few inches of it in front and behind his mitten. That short piece of rope seemed to be suspended in the white, as if it didn't go anywhere. He was sure that if he let go and stepped back even a foot or two he'd never find the rope again.

When the snow let up, Peter went out to inspect their surroundings. Drifted snow was feet deep in the lee of the trees, and behind the house and barn, but thinner out on the open ground. Short stalks of cropped wheat poked out from plowed furrows of earth, ragged gray bristles in an uneven blanket of white that extended to the horizon. In a distant patchwork of hills, the crown of one hillock was bare of snow and looked like the skull cap on the bald pate of a white-haired monk.

I'm surprised that wind didn't scour the earth, Peter thought. *It could have blown the topsoil all the way to Minnesota.*

In the spring of 1917, flush with the earnings from a couple years of bountiful harvests, Ole bought a big steam-engine tractor. "I can rent it out to my neighbors," he told Peter. "For you, it's free," he added.

Peter with Ole and his tractor (1917)

Peter and Ole went from neighbor to neighbor, renting out the tractor and hiring the men needed to plow and disk the earth and plant the fields, the ground still damp from the winter snows. Lena hired out as cook for the crew.

"That first fall, back in 1912, I had to build that sod house before the ground froze and winter set in," Ole told Peter. "The next spring I hired a tractor and a six-bladed plow to break the ground. The tractor was as big as a locomotive, even bigger than the one I bought, with metal wheels taller than a horse. It was the only way to turn the thick sod. Even then, I only turned fifty acres before we needed to plant. After the harvest, I turned another hundred and another hundred in 1915. This last fall I turned twenty-five acres, but we'll need to pick rocks before we disk it. Then we'll plant flax for a season or two, it does well on new-turned earth."

"It's hard to imagine equipment bigger than that monster," Peter said, nodding toward Ole's hulking, hissing steam-driven tractor. He and Ole hooked-up a couple of disk harrows to the rumbling behemoth. Even after four growing seasons, Ole felt at least one pass of the disk harrows was needed to break up reluctant chunks of sod that lurked in the furrows.

Peter's awe didn't lessen when they switched the disk harrow for two eight-foot wide seed drills. "Ole, I had no idea what it took," he said in wonder. He had never been around for the planting, only for the harvest.

Mostly, the two men planted wheat and, at Ole's urging, that small field of flax. "They're getting good money for flax seed," he said.

The seeds were planted and over the next few weeks the seedlings sprouted in the earth still damp from the melt of winter's snow. Lena and the girls were awe-struck as spring transformed the colorless winter landscape that had greeted them when they arrived the previous December. Now soft green field of wheat and prairie grasses, with wildflowers in bright yellow and white blanketed the rolling hills. The trees along the road celebrated the end of winter with leaves of fresh green. Everyone's spirits were high with expectation.

But the spring rains never came. Yes, the grain sprouted and grew. Hildur, not yet seven, thought the trial field of flax looked like a Minnesota lake, waves of blue rolling in the wind. But the wheat languished, the summer rains scattered and infrequent.

In early August, Peter and Ole stood in a field of wheat, a patchy expanse of golden grain, wilted stubble, and bare ground. Peter watched as Ole grasped the stem of a maturing plant between his fingers and pulled upward, striping the kernels from the head. He pressed and rolled the few seeds that filled his hand between his thumb and palm. "Another week," he said. "Then it will be ready—what there is of it." He held up a stalk of wheat and shook his head as he showed it to Peter. "Look at this. Last year the heads were as long as my finger, with more kernels than I could count. This year…" He covered the head with the width of his thumb.

Peter pulled a stalk from the dry ground and mimicked Ole, drawing it through his own fingers. "What do you think?" he asked.

"It's going to be a bad year," Ole said. "The last two years we got almost twenty-five bushels an acre. This is going to be much less than that. It's the worst I've seen."

"How have you done over the years?" Peter asked.

"This is my fifth year," Ole said. "The first two were okay, a little short of rain but we did okay. The last two years, you were here so you know, we had bumper crops. This year, it's been too dry."

Transient workers were already starting to arrive from Minnesota and Wisconsin. Others would be coming from points both east and west. In growing numbers, they were living in rooming houses in town or in tents pitched in Comertown's city park, waiting for the harvest to begin.

When the harvest started, Peter and Ole and other landowners worked alongside the itinerants, moving from farm to farm, following Ole's big tractor that pulled Peter's cousin Ole Hjelm's huge threshing machine. The big thresher, powered by the tractor, was set up just off the road at the edge of the field. Horse-drawn wagons went out into the wheat fields to collect shocks of grain that were laid out in long rows by the binder. One overflowing wagon after another was brought back to the thresher where the sheaves were fed into its gaping hopper. The machine roared and screeched as it striped off the seeds—spewing a too thin stream of golden grain into horse drawn wagons and yellow straw into huge mounds. Clouds of gritty dust billowed into the air where it wafted on the wind, working its insidious, itchy way into the clothes, hair and eyes of anyone downwind. Housewives knew not to hang out their laundry on days when the thresher was visiting.

Lena worked as a cook, with Clara as her helper, preparing five calorie-laden meals a day for the work crew, fifteen to twenty scruffy but appreciative vagabonds dressed in bib-overalls and floppy felt hats. She served a big breakfast of eggs, flapjacks, bacon and coffee. That was followed by a mid-morning lunch, a big meal again at noon, a mid-afternoon lunch, and a full meal in the evening—including pie for dessert. All the meals were prepared and served in a wood-framed cook car mounted on steel wheels so it could be moved from farm to farm, following the threshing machine. Lena did all her cooking on a cast iron cook stove crunched into the far end of the car. The workmen, twenty at a time, ate at long counters along the walls.

After the harvest, Peter and Ole drove the loaded grain wagons into Comertown where they sold the crop to the local farmers' elevator. They were paid in cash. They got a good price per bushel, the demand was still high in Europe, but the yield was only about five bushels an acre, only twenty percent of last year.

Peter was very disappointed, but remained stoic in front of Ole. Without much conversation, the two men lined the wagons with burlap before they visited the local mercantile. When they returned to the farm they had enough coal for the winter and sacks of feed for the animals, as well as sacks of flour and oatmeal and other staples for the kitchen. After Peter paid Ole his wages and the rent he owed for the year, he and Lena counted the money they had left. They shook their heads in unison. "You made more when you worked the harvest," Lena said.

"And we still need to hire the equipment and crew to plow the fields before winter sets in, and again in the spring," Peter said weakly. "It's a good thing Ole lets us use his tractor or we couldn't afford it."

Lena nodded her head. "Next year has got to be better."

Not all Peter's neighbors were even that optimistic. In fact, Peter earned a little extra money that fall as an auctioneer, selling off farm equipment and household goods for those who had already given up. One neighbor had mortgaged his homestead so he could buy more land and equipment, but hadn't made enough money to cover the payments.

Had he been back in Minnesota after the harvest, Peter would have turned his attention to hunting, shooting a deer and a few partridge to fill out the larder. But here he had taken his deer rifle down from its rack only a couple of times since their move. He often saw deer and antelope, but they were wary creatures and were usually at too great a distance. Out in this open country most hunters used long rifles with an accuracy range two to three times greater than his Winchester .30-30. He had to rely on his stealth and cunning.

Throughout the summer Peter had noticed that a small family of mule deer regularly followed a trail through the trees west of the house. He paid attention to how often they appeared, what direction they traveled, and at what time of day. When he was ready, he got up earlier than usual and placed himself at the end of the grove, made sure the wind was right, and waited for the deer to come to him. He was able to bag a couple of animals before they caught on. He gave up trying to shoot an antelope. They were skittish and unpredictable and he was never able to get close enough for a good shot.

To fill out the store, he and Ole butchered a cow and a couple of pigs, and Lena tended a good size flock of chickens, including a dozen laying hens. They wouldn't go hungry. But Peter missed hunting and the satisfaction he got from living off the land.

Lena shared Peter's disappointment with the profits from their year of hard labor and she understood the implications better than he. "It *has* to be better next year," she said, "or we can't continue."

Lena still had not come to terms with this open land, but she had only a couple of days to dwell on her unease, and what it all meant, before she had to turn her attention to her garden: drying herbs, curing and sacking potatoes, and putting up preserves for what she knew would be another long, cold winter.

29

PAINFUL RECOLLECTIONS

Aunt Claire shook her head. "They had such great hopes and that first year in Montana was such a disappointment. The rains never came. But they were very pragmatic people and they never complained or even talked about it, but we knew. At least I knew. I worked so closely with my mother, helping her in the cook car and all."

"And then came 1918, the year of the flu epidemic. And again, we had drought."

"I wonder how you all survived," I said. "As the camp cook, your mom must have been exposed to everything, every bug that came through town." I paused as I rolled that thought around in my head. "When I think of it," I continued, "maybe that's why she had such a strong immune system. And I think she passed it on to her family. I don't recall my mom ever being sick. Well, I take that back. I remember one time I was looking for her. I poked my head into her bedroom. There she was, in bed and sick for sure, but she was more hurt and upset that nobody had paid her any attention. I felt really guilty and went to the kitchen and got her a piece of toast and a glass of 7-Up, just like she'd done for me when I was sick."

"Yes," Claire said, "we were all pretty sturdy people. I do think we got it from my mother, she had an iron will and a constitution to match."

"Maybe it's because you all lived in the country, mixing with all those farm animals and grubbing in the earth. I've heard that people raised like that build up pretty strong immunity. Whatever the reason, I'm grateful. I wouldn't be here if you all hadn't survived."

"I don't know," said Claire. "Maybe you're right. All I know is that it was scary and horrible. Thankfully, we never got ill, but all around us people were sick and dying. Have I told you that my mother was a hero?"

"No. I've never heard that. Tell me about it."

"Well, as I said, it was a hard year…"

30

HEARTACHE AND HEROICS

Lena stood in her garden, her hands cupped over the top of a hoe. *I can't remember being happier for spring to come,* she thought. Lena had no argument with Ole when he said the winter had been hard. But now, in the spring of 1918, the snow had melted and dainty wildflowers tenaciously poked their heads up through the patches of dense prairie grass that hadn't been plowed under. The rolling fields had been planted and light green sprouts pushed an inch or two out of the brown soil, optimistically reaching for the sun. The fields were carpeted in a delicate shade of green, such a relief from the drab colorless winter.

Lena could now hang the laundry out in the sun, although she had to use double the clothes pins to keep her underwear from blowing into the next county. And as the weather warmed, it was so pleasant to be outdoors tilling the garden and planting the seedlings she'd started in the hotbox outside the cabin door. She still had plenty of last fall's potatoes and preserves in the root cellar. She'd had a good harvest last summer but not because of God's good graces. She had watched in frustration as low dark clouds passed overhead, so full of promise. Or worse yet, when she watched, with conflicting feelings of envy and guilt, curtains of rain just over the distant rise, watering someone else's garden, but not hers. She had carried pail after pail of water from the well to keep her garden growing. She would do everything needed to assure another good harvest this year.

As Lena leaned on her hoe, lost in a moment of reverie, Hildur, now seven going-on-eight, emerged from the house trailed by her father. "Daddy and I are going to visit the trees. Do you want to come?"

Lena looked toward the cottonwoods that traced the road, their leaves still a delicate spring green. "No," she said. "I have too much work to do. You go with your father. But don't be gone too long. You need to help with the laundry."

"We won't," Hildur said as she grabbed Peter's hand. "Come on, Daddy."

Hildur and Peter followed the edge of the road toward the trees, chasing their long shadows, the morning sun lighting the hills to the west with a golden light. "It's so pretty," Hildur said. "Can we find our favorite spot?"

"Lead the way," Peter replied.

Hildur walked on ahead, followed the margin of the stand of trees for a ways, then ducked under a low-hanging limb and disappeared into the underbrush. Peter bent down low and followed his daughter into a small shaded opening where she was already sitting on an aged fallen log, its silvered bark curled back just enough to allow a father and daughter to sit side-by-side.

As Peter settled down next to her, Hildur said, "Tell me a story, Daddy."

"Okay," Peter began. "Once upon a time there was a good little girl and her name was Hildur."

Hildur giggled.

"Little Hildur loved to sit on a log in the woods under a big tree. She liked the cool shade and the smell of the earth. She could sit quietly for hours, not saying a word, just watching the sun through the leaves and listening to the birds singing."

Hildur placed her small hand on the back of Peter's. They sat that way for nearly half an hour until Hildur gave a sigh and said, "We need to get back to help Mommy."

Still in her garden, Lena drew the hoe, breaking up a small clump of soil. She paused to watch her daughter lead Peter out of the trees and back toward the house. *Yes, it is a good spring day,* she thought.

Over the long winter, in the dim light inside their sod home, Lena and Peter had talked about their disappointment with their profits from last year's harvest. Peter had worked hard in the fields all spring and summer and they had both worked to exhaustion during the harvest. They had some cash, but it was so much less than they had expected. They weren't as well off as they had been back in Minnesota. They both knew the crops had to be better than last year, but even Peter, who was always the optimist, had his doubts.

In late April, Brita and her son, Nels, were bedridden with a bad case of the flu. Lena drove Ole's buggy over to the Nass place; she was concerned they might get pneumonia, but after a couple of weeks they rallied. She brought several meals to feed the family and helped keep the house orderly until Brita was back on her feet. Ole reported that a couple of families in Comertown had been laid low as well.

May and June dragged on hot and dry. Lena knew they needed rain by the amount of water she had to pump each day to keep her garden growing. In late June, Peter announced that the wheat was stressed and the heads spare. It was already clear that the harvest would be thin, no better than last year.

Then in July, Peter read an article in a newspaper Ole had brought from town. "People are sick and dying back east," he told Lena. "There's some kind of influenza, they say."

"I'm glad that's not what we had here," Lena said, thinking of Brita, Nels, and the families in town.

But it likely was the same illness, just a milder version. Beginning that spring and stretching through the next winter, Montana experienced three waves of the Spanish Influenza, each more virulent than the last. It all started a thousand miles away, in Kansas, back in February while Peter and his family were hunkering down against Montana's bitter winter.

A local doctor in Kansas reported that several people in and around Haskell County had come down with severe flu and a half-dozen had died.²² A month later, several young men at Camp Funston, three hundred miles west of Haskell, became sick. The outbreak spread rapidly among the 56,000 men who were jammed together in the overcrowded camp—the second-largest army training camp in the country. The men had been short of blankets and warm clothing during one of the worst winters recorded. In March a camp cook reported ill. Within three weeks, more than eleven hundred soldiers were sick enough to be in the hospital. Uncounted others sought treatment at infirmaries distributed around the base.

Soldiers from Camp Funston were assigned to other Army installations or allowed to visit their hometowns scattered throughout the region before they were shipped off to France to fight in the War-to-End-All-Wars raging in Europe. They carried illness and death wherever they went.

The second wave of illness to hit Montana started in August, likely spurred on by the influx of dozens of itinerant workers arriving for the harvest. The work crews were the first to succumb, especially the younger men in their twenties and thirties. Many in that age bracket had joined the Army, but not all. The symptoms came on fast—fever, headache, and nausea—and progressed swiftly to nosebleeds, congestion and violent coughing. Pneumonia was common, with the lungs of the sick filling so quickly that many drowned in their own fluids.

Peter and Ole and the other farmers in the area struggled to cobble together crews of men healthy enough to work the harvest. Lena saw men arrive for breakfast and fall ill by noon. Volunteers came from Comertown with wagons to haul the sick back to town where they could be cared for. The Westby schoolhouse was turned into a hospital.²³

Early in the harvest a local man approached Lena as she was dishing out breakfast. "Lena," he said, his voice pleading. "I'm worried. My wife is sick, and the neighbor lady is too. Do you know anyone who can help?"

"I'll ride home with you this evening. I'll see what we can do."

Over the next several weeks, Lena cooked for the field hands during the day and in the evening visited one or another family in distress. She nursed the sick—and cooked and cleaned—then got a ride home. Then Lena did it all again the next day, and the next. Some of the neighbor women volunteered to help—giving Lena a hand in the cook car and handling some of the home visits. Ole fell sick, too, and Peter tried his best to manage the household.

It wasn't until late September, when most of the itinerant workers had left, that the number of sick began to subside. Several of the workers and one local woman had died. Others had made it through the worst of the illness and were slowly recovering. Lena was exhausted and thankful that her family had been spared.

Late one Sunday morning, a beautiful fall day in October, Lena looked out the window to see a dozen people walking up the road toward her sod home. Several buggies were parked out by the main road, the horses standing quietly, their noses buried deep into feed sacks.

"What's this?" she said to Peter and Ole, who were sitting at the kitchen table drinking coffee after their morning chores. Clara was reading a book to Anna, Hildur and Selma.

Peter and Ole stood and joined Lena at the window.

"Don't know," said Ole.

"Me either," said Peter. "Let me find out."

Peter stepped outside. The day was cool and unusually calm; the sun bright in the cloudless sky. "Good morning," Peter said, as he surveyed the crowd. He recognized the faces—men and women and a few children, all neighbors. Brita and Andrew and Nels led the way, all carrying what looked like food. Vera was there too.

"Lena," Brita called. "Please come out."

Lena stepped outside and stood next to Peter. Ole stood in the doorway with the children peeking from the shadows.

"Lena," Brita said. 'We are here to thank you for all you've done for us these last few weeks. We all agree you are an angel."

Lena was surprised and embarrassed.

Peter saw tears well-up in Lena's eyes, one of the few times he'd seen that happen in all the years of their marriage. He put a hand on her shoulder.

"We've brought food," Brita said. "We want to share a meal with you."

"Welcome, welcome," Peter said as he invited them inside with a sweep of his hand.

There was barely enough room inside for everyone, but Brita knew exactly what to do. She led the way, set the food she brought on the kitchen table and beckoned the others to follow her example. Coffee pots were placed on the stove, casseroles and baskets of bread and tubs of butter were uncovered. Stacks of plates, and cups, and a basket of utensils were set out on the sideboard. A full-blown smorgasbord and celebration were underway.

Lena was overcome and unusually quiet, barely able to mutter an occasional thank you.

Peter beamed.

As people began to take dessert, Peter looked at Lena. "Should I tell them?" he whispered.

She nodded her head.

"Please, everyone," Peter said in his stage voice. "May I have your attention?"

The crowd quieted and turned toward him, their faces expectant.

"I know Lena is very grateful for your warm friendship. Right now she seems speechless. Let me say on her behalf that she's glad she was able to help and is so happy to see you all healthy." Peter paused as those in the crowd nodded their heads. "And with such good appetites," he added, and the crowd laughed.

"We both value your friendship," he continued, "but Lena and I have an announcement. We will not be staying on. I've talked to Ole, who has been like part of our family these last two years. We are giving Ole his house back and we will be heading back to Minnesota in a couple of weeks."

In November, as the Backs packed up their things and headed back to Minnesota, the flu outbreak resumed with renewed virulence. Someone died nearly every day that month in and around the northeast corner of Montana. Then the number of sick subsided, but briefly—the illness not quite as ready to leave Montana as the Backs. In December the flu surged back with a vengeance in a wave of sickness and death that persisted through the next spring.

Most flus strike hardest at the young and the elderly, but this flu disproportionately sought out those in their twenties and thirties. Some estimate that eight to ten percent of young adults then living were killed by the virus. In absolute numbers, the epidemic killed more people than the infamous plague that wiped out a quarter of Europe's population in the fourteenth century.[24]

In northeast Montana, locals weren't sure who or what to blame for the flu's virulence, the origins of the disease still unknown. On October 22, 1918, at the height of the epidemic and less than three weeks before the end of the Great War, an article in the *Plentywood Herald* surmised, with dark patriotic sarcasm, that many of the deaths attributed to the Spanish Flu should really be attributed to the "German Influenza, which was very epidemic in nature [especially in Europe], and has been spread mostly by disloyal pro-Germans, socialists, and non-partisan agitators." The article went on to say that, "It can be prevented from spreading …by buying Liberty Bonds, War Savings Stamps …donating liberally to the Red Cross [and taking in the] contents of the *Producers News* and voting for loyal American candidates." [25]

By the time the influenza pandemic had run its course, over 5,000 people had died in Montana alone. There were more than 500,000 deaths across America and at least 21 million worldwide. Because so many remote corners of the world went uncounted, some experts estimate that the worldwide death count may have been closer to 50 million or even 100 million.

Peter and Lena were not the only ones to give up on Montana. And bad as it was, it wasn't the flu that ended Montana's land rush. After a promising beginning, homesteader dreams began to fracture in 1917. In that year and for several years to follow, drought, rust, hail, and grasshoppers, or some combination of them all, resulted in poor harvests. And with the end of the Great War, grain prices dropped. Many homesteaders found they couldn't make a go of it and went bankrupt or sold their claims to more optimistic neighbors or to new arrivals. Many moved to points west or, like the Backs, went back east.[26]

Even with an occasional good year, there was no way the economy of the area could fully recover. The land and weather were not well suited to dryland agriculture. Native grasses, nutritious but slow-growing, had sustained roaming bison herds for centuries but could not replenish themselves fast enough to keep up with the concentrated over-grazing of cattle. Then, in 1929, a little over a decade after the Back family gave up on Montana, a poor crop year colluded with the November stock market crash to set the stage for a decade of depression.

Peter and Lena were lucky to get out when they did. That fragile land with its uncertain weather in the northeast corner of Montana never did regain its earlier glory. Small farmers and small towns struggled and died and the railroads failed. Even so, Ole Hellegaard, a tenacious Norwegian bachelor farmer, persisted.

31

NEXT-YEAR COUNTRY

A century after the Back's retreat, Sue and I took a sojourn up to northeast Montana. I wanted to see the country first hand and to stand where my grandparents stood so many decades earlier. It was late June and the rolling countryside was more vibrant and lush than I had imagined. The vast green fields of wheat that dominated the landscape during the Back's era are still common but are now augmented by broad swaths of breathtakingly iridescent chartreuse, fields carpeted in small white-flowers, and acres of sweet-smelling buffalo grass, clover and hay.

We spent a day in Scobey, a small town several miles to the west of Comertown, our destination. Scobey was once the largest distribution point for wheat in the world and now hosts the Daniels County Museum and Frontier Village. We attended "Pioneer Days," a popular celebration held each year during the last weekend in June. We started the morning eating breakfast in an authentic wood-sided cook car like the one my grandmother staffed a hundred years ago. We each had an eye-opening mug of dark coffee, although Sue would have preferred decaffeinated. We ate flapjacks drizzled with chokecherry syrup and saucer-sized patties of zesty country sausage.

After breakfast we walked among giant rusted threshing machines—all cranks and levers and chutes—their knobbed wrought-iron wheels anchored deep in tufts of prairie grass. I compared my height against the massive metal wheel of an old steam-driven tractor and stared in awe at a sturdy sodbuster plow with six plowshares. We walked the boardwalk and explored the numerous buildings that had been moved to the museum's pioneer village: a one room school house, a farmhouse, a mercantile and pharmacy, a blacksmith shop, and a saloon—among others. I was a little disappointed that they didn't have a sod house like the one my grandparents lived in, but they did have a couple of grayed and neglected, yet-to-be-restored, proving-up cabins (the small cabins built by settlers to prove their homestead claims).

I was amused and enlightened by the conversations I overheard—big-handed guys as old as me, wearing ball caps and faded blue jeans cinched tight with big belt buckles, talking about the weather. "We got some good rain but it's not enough," one said. And, "We didn't get any up near us. But I could see them clouds go'en by. Maybe next year," said another. I was told by a longtime local that northeast Montana is often called "Next- Year" country. "Next year we'll get more rain. Next year will be better."

At one o'clock there was a reenactment of a bank robbery—gunshots and all—the area was known for hosting a number of cattle and horse thieves and other outlaws back in its day. Mid-afternoon, with a light rain falling that no one complained about, we watched a parade of restored antique automobiles and rumbling and wheezing tractors. As the rain abated, we filed into the REX theater to watch the *Dirty Shame Show*—a burlesque show featuring music, skits, and dance performed by local talent. The show culminated in an enthusiastic and remarkably well-choreographed rendition of the can-can. It was all a hoot.

Late in the evening the clouds began to clear and, anticipating a colorful sunset, I drove to the western edge of town to a spot with an unobstructed view of the horizon. I wasn't disappointed. As the sun dropped out of sight, the steel blue clouds overhead began to take on color, transitioning from a pale pink, then a rosy salmon, and then on to a bold iridescent orange crisscrossed with streaks of gold and purple. The horizon was flushed with a pure light, foretelling clear skies in the morning.

Early the next morning I shared a cup of coffee with the owner of our motel. His family had settled near Scobey at about the same time as my grandparents. "In June," he told me, "it's hard to tell how the wheat is doing. From the road the crop might look okay but rain is needed for the heads to fully mature. Lack of rain may not kill the crop altogether but the heads will be small. In a good year you can get twenty-five bushel an acre. With a few good years your profits can carry you over a bad year or two when you might yield only five or ten bushels an acre, or none."

"What were those brightly flowered fields we saw?" I asked.

"The bright yellow-green flowers are probably canola, it's like rapeseed, for canola oil. The little white flowers are probably pulses—red lentils and peas. They do better with uncertain rain."

"What about flax?"

"Flax is good," he replied. "It's the crop of choice for newly turned soil. It helps break it up and it changes the chemistry. Profits are good, too."

With our coffee cups drained and our conversation coming to a close, I said, "We're driving over to Comertown this morning. Any place between here and there to get breakfast on a Sunday?"

"There's not much between here and there any day of the week." He replied. "But there is one place, a good one, too. It's a bar in Flaxville, the *Bum Steer*. Most Sundays we go there ourselves."

It was a little after eight in the morning when we drove into Flaxville. The *Bum Steer* wasn't clearly marked but still wasn't hard to find—it was the only building on the town's block-long main street that could serve as a bar. We parked by the front door, the only car on the street, unsure the place was open. "Well, let's see," I said, as I tried the door. It was unlocked.

The lights were on but the place was empty except for a middle-aged woman near the kitchen door leaning on the end of the massive wood bar that dominated the room. The woman said welcome and upon my probing told us she had inherited the establishment from her father who had bought the place back in 1983. She was the owner, bartender, cook, and chief-bottle-washer. "Help's hard to find around here," she told us. "And I'm open every day except Thanksgiving, Christmas and Easter. It's a living."

I admired the long dark wood back-bar with a stretch of big mirrors anchored by strong columns on each end. The head of a long-horned steer, sculpted artfully in a burnished metal, hung in the center above the mirrors. "Was that back-bar brought in from somewhere?" I asked.

"No. It was built right here, back in 1912. It was painted over when Dad bought the place and he striped it back to its natural wood."

As we talked, a reedy-limbed elderly fellow walked in, nodded at us and asked the owner for change. She gave him several dollar bills which he took over to one of the six big gaming machines that hunkered in one corner of the room. He slipped a bill into the machine and started playing electronic poker.

As the owner took our breakfast order, I asked her what she liked best about living here.

"I love the freedom and the open land. I don't much like the mountains and I don't like living in the city."

Her answer helped explain the Anheuser Busch poster she had displayed on one wall: "To hell with your mountains, show me your Busch."

Her penchant for wide open spaces got me to thinking about my grandparents. They were people of the forest, most at home in the sheltering limbs of surrounding trees. They must have felt exposed and vulnerable out here. Place is important and what you like is what you know.

That thought reminded me of a story I'd first heard years earlier when I was working in Uzbekistan. There were two cousins. One lived among the mountain-juniper forests near Surkhan. The other lived on the vast and open dry plains of Amudarya. One year the cousin from the forest took the long trip to visit his dry-plains cousin, bringing a tree as a gift. The dry-plains cousin thanked his benefactor and together they planted the tree and gave it a good watering. Years later, the cousin from the forest came back for another visit but could find no trace of the tree. "What happened?" he asked. "Well," his cousin replied. "I watered it religiously and it grew into a splendid tree. The shade was nice, but I cut it down. It spoiled the view."

While I was occupied with my thoughts, a couple entered and sat on high stools at the long bar and two guys came in, ordered Bloody Marys, and sat down at the table next to us. The owner greeted each of the customers by name and asked if they wanted the usual. They nodded and she disappeared into the kitchen.

One of the fellows at the next table asked us, "Where you from in Colorado?" He had obviously noticed our car and out-of-state license plate.

"Fort Collins," Sue answered.

"Around here you know everybody," he said. "Everybody knows you and your truck and they know where you've been and where you're going. You don't have to use your turn signal."

Just then, as if to illustrate his point, a fellow in a ball cap emerged from the kitchen. "You cooking this morning, Bill?" our neighbor asked him. "No," Bill chuckled. "Just came in through the back door."

By now a family with a couple of kids had settled at another table. The place was filling up and we decided we should make room. We paid our bill, gave our thanks to the proprietor and stepped out onto the street. Another car pulled up and parked. We exchanged hellos as they entered the bar.

"Busy place," I said to Sue.

"Yes," Sue replied, "and everybody we've met is so friendly. But there's no way you can get a cup of decaffeinated coffee around here."

We drove on toward Comertown, following back roads that weren't on the map but I'd researched on Google Earth before we'd left home. There was no telephone service out where we were and few signs that the countryside was still inhabited except long stretches of barbwire fence that follow the roadway. We saw an occasional dilapidated shack or barn of weather-worn and silvered wood, long abandoned and leaning away from the prevailing winds.

Comertown is on the map but only as a memory. A couple of

abandoned buildings still stand on a rise above the road and a long slab of concrete, the foundation of once towering grain elevators, lies prostrate next to the abandoned railroad tracks. We followed the old dirt East Comertown Road to where it intersects with North Star Road. We turned north and drove five miles where we intersected with Ueland Road that runs east-west between sections, just two miles shy of the Canadian border. Straddling the road was the plot of land we were looking for, the original Hellegaard homestead, sitting in a broad grassy bowl, three miles across from lip to lip.

I walked out on the plot where Ole Hellegaard's sod house once stood. The scenery probably hasn't changed much in a hundred years, and yet it has. No farmhouses or barns can be seen anywhere in the wide shallow basin. A thin copse of trees, where my mother sat quietly with her father and Peter hunted deer, still traces a line across the valley floor. The most dramatic difference is the number of pumpjacks, oil rigs, scattered across the landscape—their huge weighted heads ponderously rising and falling like dinosaurs sating their hunger on the viscus remains of their prehistoric ancestors. We drove into the gravel driveway of the "Hellegaard Battery" where large earth-colored tanks collect petroleum from a web of nearby pumpjacks.

The small Hellegaard homestead is still held by the family, now cobbled together with other farms and leased lands into a large family company that runs cattle behind fences, plants hay and grain hoping for good weather, and collects royalty checks from the big oil company that taps the mineral riches that lie beneath their grazing cattle and uncertain crops.

Long stretches of abandoned railroad track wend through the vast landscape, crossed here and there by washboard dirt roads that were once major intersections for commerce now long gone. The railroad tracks once connected to other tracks that networked throughout the region and linked the now lonesome land to the rest of the continent..

Northeastern Montana has not been easy for the people who have lived there during the last hundred years and it isn't easy for those who live there now. Still, the locals hold to the promise of next year with stoic optimism. Ole Hellegaard was one of those that held on. In 1923 he gave up his bachelor life and married Margret Olson. They had three children who eventually expanded the size of their holding—and retained the mineral rights.

Lena and Peter Back weren't so tenacious. In November 1918, at the end of a year of flu and another poor harvest, they gathered their children, packed up all they owned, and boarded a train headed back to Minnesota.

32

BROKEN DREAMS

It was a cold and overcast day in mid-November of 1918 when the Back family arrived in Kelliher. It was just days after the end of the Great War that left nine million soldiers dead and twenty-one million wounded—not counting the millions who died of illness or starvation.[27] The Backs arrived at the train station travel-weary, disappointed, and broke—but back home in Minnesota. Peter's brother, Otto Hjelm, met them with a wagon.

"You won't like what you'll find," Otto told Peter and Lena. "Your place has been trashed by hunters. You won't be able to live there until it's fixed up. We'll stop by on our way to our place. You can stay with us until you decide what to do."

Peter's heart sank. He had been so eager to be back home.

Lena pursed her lips and shook her head. "Let's see," she said.

Once they were on the road Otto announced, "There's more bad news. Peter Olson died."

"Oh no!" Lena said. He was her stepbrother and had been the mail carrier in the area for several years. "What happened?"

"He bought a Ford Model T last year and this spring he drove it into a ditch. It turned over and he drowned."

"Damn those county commissioners," muttered Peter. *Katrina had said he was thinking about buying a car,* he thought. *She told me when she delivered Selma.* "Those damn county commissioners," he repeated. "I knew something like this was going to happen. I almost slipped a sled runner into a ditch myself, more than once."

"What's Johanna going to do?" Lena asked.

"She couldn't make it out here on her own, not with eight children," Otto said. "She moved into Bemidji. She's working at the Bagley mill loading lumber."

Peter nodded his head. "She's stronger than most men I know, me included."

When they reached the Back homestead, Otto parked the wagon on the road while Peter and Lena walked back to the cabin. The pathway was nearly overgrown and strewn with fallen branches. The cabin door was off its hinges and leaning against an outside wall. There were empty cans and piles of trash scattered about. The cooking stove was gone and the kitchen window was broken. The casting on the heating stove was cracked and the door was missing. Several treads were missing from the stairway up to the loft. Some animal, maybe a raccoon, had been living up there and perhaps still was.

"We can't live here this winter," Lena said. "It will take weeks of work and money we don't have to get it back in shape. And we don't have any provisions. It's just too much."

"You're right," said Peter. "And we don't have any firewood or a place to burn it if we did."

As they walked back to the wagon, Peter kicked a branch that lay across the path. *It has been such a hard year, and now this.*

"You can stay with us until you decide what to do," Otto repeated. He urged the horses forward and gave Peter and Lena a few minutes to let their minds settle before adding, "I've heard they need a cook at the logging camp. They could probably use another lumberjack too. If you're interested, we can check into it."

Peter and Lena worked the nearby logging camp that winter. Working as a cook at a logging camp was a different experience for Lena. She had done a lot of cooking for a lot of men over the years, but the lumberjacks were a rough bunch and often crude. She was embarrassed when her long red hair attracted wolf whistles. *I'm the mother of five children*, she thought. She tried to straighten her curls with sugar water, but it was such a mess that she finally started tucking her bun inside a white cotton bonnet.

Otto agreed to put up Clara, Anna, and Hildur for the season so they could attend school in Waskish. Vera, now thirteen, got a job as a cook and maid with a family in Bemidji.

The next spring, 1919, after the logging camp closed for the season and the road was dry enough to travel, Peter and Lena revisited the homestead. Over the winter Peter's memory of the damage he'd seen in the fall had faded and he began to convince himself that it wouldn't be too hard to repair the place. But as he surveyed all that needed to be done he realized it was actually far worse than he remembered. In addition to the cabin, the barn was missing some of its siding. Some animal, maybe a bear, had wintered in the root cellar. Two of the wells had been left uncovered and the fence surrounding Lena's garden was in tatters. Peter shook his head. "It came apart so quickly," he whispered.

Lena wasn't sure if he was referring to the destruction of their property or their dream. Lena thought he might cry. "I'm sorry Peter," she said, "but even if we started up again, it was never going to get better. I think our life here is done."

"It's not even worth paying the taxes," Peter said. He knew his dream to be independent, supporting his family with his own labor, on his own land, was over. *This was sorry land to begin with*, he thought. "I made a mistake," he said to Lena.

"Don't blame yourself," she said. "I wanted it, too."

"What do we do now?" Peter said. "This is all I know."

"You're a hard worker, Peter," Lena said, placing her hand on Peter's elbow. "So am I."

They both stood looking at the destruction. "We'll find a way," Lena whispered.

"Yes," Peter said. But at the moment he wasn't so sure.

A few days later Peter and Otto returned from a trip to Kelliher. "The county is building a road from Kelliher to Shotley," Peter announced. "They need extra hands and a cook."

For the next two summers Peter and Lena worked for the county road crew. In the winter they again worked at the logging camp.

In the late summer of 1920 they received word that Peter's mother, Christina Hjelm, had died in Holmes City, two months short of her seventy-seventh birthday. They had last seen her four years earlier when they picked up Clara on their way to Montana.

Peter and Lena left the girls with Lena's sister, Katrina, and joined Peter's brothers on the train to Alexandria and Holmes City. The funeral was not as sad an affair as Peter expected. Both he and Lena had so many relatives there, many of whom they had not seen in years. And there was food, lots of food.

Peter talked to several of his cousins who had never been able to find a homestead and were now working for local businesses. Another cousin was there from Montana. "I gave up my farm," he told Peter. "A lot of people are leaving. It's so uncertain. Drought can wipe you out in a season. I think we were sold a bill-of-goods."

Peter nodded his head. He didn't need any convincing.

Peter and Lena returned to Waskish, again working at the logging camp and on the road crew. When Hildur was in sixth grade and Anna in seventh they were sent to Kelliher to join Clara who was living there with a family and attending the local school.

"My husband's dead," Katrina Chellson cried, "shot and killed in the woods."

It was the fall of 1922 and Lena and Peter stood open-mouthed as they listened to Katrina's story.

"Was it a hunting accident?" asked Peter.

"Yes. No," Katrina stammered. "He was taking a shortcut through the woods, following a deer trail over on our neighbor's place. He was shot in a deer trap and died before they could get him to the doctor."

It was a week after the accident but the Backs, no longer living on the homestead, were just hearing the news. Lena held Katrina as she wept.

Peter heard later that the neighbor had strapped a rifle to a tree and set up a trip-wire, hoping to shoot a deer. Pete Chellson had stumbled into the trap. When the neighbor heard the shot he came running with a wheel barrow, ready to haul the deer back to his house.

"Have you decided what you're going to do?" asked Lena.

"I don't know yet," Katrina replied.

The next summer, in June of 1923, Vera came up from Bemidji for a visit and to celebrate her eighteenth birthday. She had a young man in tow, Delbert Hall, the man she would soon marry.

During their visit Lena announced, "We're moving into town, too. Our family has been too scattered these last few years. We can put all the girls in school there."

Lena didn't yet know, but she was pregnant.

33

EMBARRASSED

"I heard you were an unexpected child," I said to Uncle Glenn. "Tell me about that."

"Well first," he said, "my mother didn't want to admit she was pregnant with me. I was born ten years after Sally (Selma). Mom was embarrassed. When she started to show, she quit her job and stayed at home. Nobody knew, not even Elvera. Del, Elvera's husband-to-be, saw the doctor's car parked in front of the house and went in to find out who was sick. Mom wasn't sick, she had me!"

Glenn paused before continuing. "After they gave up the homestead my folks moved around a lot, finding work where they could. They were living in Bemidji when I was born."

"So I never lived in the cabin. But when I was a kid I used to go out there with my dad. He'd given up the homestead by then, like most of his neighbors. Nobody could make a go of that poor land, so they let the taxes lapse. But we would still go out there to hunt or cut wood. Dad was smart, and he knew the woods. He taught me how to shoot, and I was pretty proud of my marksmanship. When I went into the Marines they wanted to make me an instructor."

"They moved to Bemidji that fall, 1923, rented a small house, and enrolled the girls in school. Dad worked odd jobs—stacking boxes in a box factory and unloading coal cars for the railroad. I was born on February 16, 1924, delivered by a midwife. Mom was forty-four years of age and Dad was fifty-one."

Peter Back with son, Glenn (Circa 1930)

"Later that year Mom's sister, Katrina Chellson, the one whose husband had been shot, abandoned her Waskish homestead and followed our family to Bemidji. Mom was happy to have Katrina nearby even though she was too late to deliver me."

34

PAST AND FUTURE WORLDS

Like so many others, Peter and Lena gave up rural living and moved to town. An era was rapidly coming to a close. The inexorable shift from rural to urban living that played out in the first few decades of the twentieth century is arguably the most dramatic social transformation in American history. The Backs were among the last of the pioneers, citizens enticed by the Homestead Act to spread out across the vast American landscape. The very concept of homesteading was based on the assumption that small farms would be the foundation of America's future.

Undoubtedly, the homesteaders were brave and hardy souls. Their hardships and self-reliance have been romanticized by countless books, movies, and television to the point of myth and legend: the independent American, self-sufficient, succeeding by their own tenacity and hard work. But the reality was less romantic and more brutal; many homesteaders barely surviving season-to-season. Their claimed acreage was often too rocky, or too dry, or otherwise unsuitable for farming, or their parcels were too small for livestock. Many homesteaders, like my grandparents, lived a life of grueling manual labor, trapped in a cycle of perpetual poverty.

When they were introduced in the late 1800s, power tractors and plows and threshing machines made large-scale farming a possibility but the expense was beyond the financial means of all but a few. Many homesteaders were forced off their small farms as their lands were consolidated with other small parcels into large, sprawling commercial enterprises with thousands of acres under cultivation.

All across America, the lives of thousands of self-sufficient independent small farmer came to an end—only the myth remains.

And in a parallel universe, industrialization was creating jobs in the cities, drawing subsistence farmers from the slogging drag of rural poverty into the growing urban centers such as Detroit, Chicago, St. Louis, and Minneapolis.

But the Backs didn't have the interest or the skills to make the dramatic transition required to move to the Twin Cities. They were getting older and had made enough big moves—first from Sweden to America, then from Holmes City to the north woods, and then to the rolling plains of Montana—all for naught. With pragmatic resignation they moved to Bemidji, a small town with close ties to the rural life they had known, a place they knew, a town well removed from the hustle and bustle of the big city. They moved into town because they thought it would provide more opportunities, maybe a change in fortune. They got by, rented a house and found work—odd jobs and hard labor for Peter, and cooking, always cooking, for Lena. But they didn't count on the Great Depression that kept a heavy hand on any upward progress they might have longed for. It was up to their children to fulfill the dreams they harbored when they first migrated to America.

Clara was the first of the Backs to launch herself into the new world. In the summer of 1926 she moved to Minneapolis, changed her name to Claire, and began her life as a self-sufficient woman. She started by waitressing in the "big city" before moving west to work in California and the grand resorts in San Francisco and Phoenix.

The fall after Claire left for Minneapolis, Hildur and Anna entered eighth grade together. They graduated from high school in the spring of 1929. Later that summer Hildur followed her older sister, Claire, and moved to Minneapolis with ambitions to attend nursing school. She was barely settled when she found work as a housekeeper and babysitter, much as her mother had done when she first arrived in Holmes City in 1902, fresh off the boat from Sweden.

Hildur didn't notice when the stock market crashed that fall, nor did Claire, who was in California at the time. Peter and Lena did, although they didn't know it as the "Great Depression" until years later. They did know that work was hard to find.

Peter gritted his teeth and applied for a job dynamiting stumps for his long-time nemesis, Beltrami County, the drainer of swamps and local taxing authority. He was turned down. "You're too old, Peter," the county work boss had said. "We've hired another man." Two weeks later the work boss came by to see Peter. "You still interested in that job?" he asked. "The man we hired had an accident. He blew off his hand."

Peter spent two years clearing land for the county and, again, Lena worked as a cook for the county poorhouse. They each earned one dollar a day and were glad to have the income. But it *was* the depression and the county was broke. Instead of giving workers cash, the county issued warrants which few local merchants would honor—except a downtown mercantile that redeemed the voucher at eighty-cents on the dollar.

In 1934 the work ran out in Bemidji and the Backs moved to the small community of Gheen to work for a road crew. The following year they moved back to Waskish where they managed the Sunset Lodge that housed and fed the road crew working on a highway being built from Kelliher to Baudette. Peter also worked with the walleye pike spawning staff, part of the fish hatchery program that stocked Red Lake and other lakes in the area with the popular game fish.

When road construction wound down in 1938, Peter and Lena moved back to Bemidji. Considering the depressed economy, they had faired pretty well. They were the proud owners of a used Chevrolet and had a little cash in their pockets. They secured a loan for $3,500 and bought a house across the street from Bemidji High School where their son Glenn played varsity basketball.

35

PASSING ON A LEGACY

"Our house was right across the street from the high school," Uncle Glenn said. "Mom told me that when times were tough, my dad wanted to take payments from the state.[28] But Mom refused. They'd put a lien on your house and you'd need to pay it back when you died. She always found a way to manage."

"I enjoyed those years," Glenn continued. "I enjoyed playing ball. We went to the state basketball tournament one year—that was a big thrill. I don't think Mom or Dad ever watched me play, but I got to spend a lot of time with them, especially my dad. That's when we went hunting together."

"Sometimes Dad and I would walk up to the Hall's store, the little log cabin grocery that Elvera and Del owned. This was before the Hall's bought the resort. It was just a few blocks from our home. Dad and I would visit with the Hall's, have a nice conversation, maybe buy an ice cream, then walk home."

"Dad died before I graduated, you know," Glenn continued. "He had a lot of pain. We took him down to the Cities where your dad got him in to see a doctor at the University of Minnesota, where your dad was working at the time. The doctor ran some tests but couldn't find anything wrong. He told my dad he just needed to eat more. A couple of months later we took him to an old rural doctor up in Bemidji. 'Mister Back,' the doctor said. 'You've got pancreatic cancer. There's not much we can do for you.'"

"Dad died the next spring, April of 1940, a few months before you were born. He was sixty-seven years old. He didn't have any money but he left Mom the house. She lived there another thirty-five years."

"Our folks had it tough, by golly," Glenn said. "And I don't think either one of them ever had a vacation. Dad was good-humored and he enjoyed being outdoors, but I don't think he ever had much fun."

"And Mom was so serious, all business, and religious—much more so than Dad. Even with her limited income, she'd give ten percent to the church. She read a lot, on history and politics. She attended concerts and lectures. She was energetic and always busy. She didn't have much patience for boredom. And she was frugal. She couldn't understand how people who made several hundred dollars a week could spend all that money."

"When I think about it, I don't think she took a vacation except to visit one of us kids until she was in her seventies. Your dad and mom took her along on a road trip out west and up into Canada. Mom didn't even have a passport. At the border, your dad told her, 'If the customs officer asks you for your passport, tell him you forgot it at home.' But Mom wouldn't lie, so on the way back she said, in her accented English, that no, she didn't have a passport. Your dad cringed but the customs officer just laughed and waved them through."

"Another time your dad asked her if she had ever been back to Sweden. She said no. Your mom helped her get a passport and your dad paid her way. I remember how thrilled she was, as excited as she ever got, and really surprised your dad would do that for her."

"I hope she had fun," I said.

"Me too," Glenn said. I could hear a catch in his voice and then a pause before he continued. "I have to tell you a story about your grandmother. She was not the most outgoing person you could know, but you could not ask for a better friend. There was an old woman who lived next door, a cranky recluse. Mom kept a watchful eye on her for years until the old lady died. Mom was the only person at her funeral."

"Mom died in that house, in January of 1974, a few weeks past her ninety-fourth birthday."

Glenn was quiet for a moment before he continued. "My folks had it pretty hard, but us Back kids did pretty well, I think. We all did better than they expected. They wanted us to get a basic education, to graduate from high school, but nobody ever suggested that we might go to college. For kids of immigrants, we did okay. And our kids did great!"

"That reminds me," Glenn continued. "Have you seen that great family photo taken of all of us Backs. We're all in it. It was a year or so before Dad died."

The Back Family (Circa 1939)
Back row: Elvera (Vera), Peter, Ann (Anna), Glenn
Front row: Claire (Clara), Lena (Caroline), Hildur, Sally (Selma)
Scherling Photography, Bemidji, Minnesota: used with permission

"Yes, I've got a copy. I love that photo. You were a good-looking bunch."

The telephone went silent for a moment. I think we were both lost in our heads.

I broke the silence. "I agree. It can be hard for immigrants, but often their children and grandchildren do pretty well."

"Yeah, I think so," Glenn continued. "I went into the Marines, got some college, and I had a really good career in banking. And look at our kids. Marilyn and I are so proud of them. And my sister Elvera, and Del, they made music together and so enjoyed the resort."

"That reminds me," I interjected. "I always thought that my experience—weeks with my cousin Tom at the resort—was unique to me. But when I interviewed my younger brothers—Steve, Dave and Bert—I was reminded that they all had spent summers at Moose Lake with one or another of our cousins who were close to them in age. Thanks to Elvera and Del's hospitality, we all grew up valuing the out-of-doors."

"As you know," Glenn said, "they never had children of their own but I think they got their parental satisfactions from nurturing a continuing parade of nephews and nieces, like you and Tom and the others."

"It's only now, in retrospect," I continued, "after learning more about Lena and Peter, that I realize how much Elvera and Del resembled your parents, more than any of the rest of you. Elvera was pragmatic and a bit stern, like your mother. She was attracted to Del because he was cheerful, like your father, and a musician to boot."

"Yes," Glenn said. "Every week during the summer season they invited all the resort guests into the main cabin for an evening of music, Elvera played the piano and Del the trombone, with everyone signing along."

"I think," I said, "their summers at the resort satisfied their love of nature and in the winters they both worked in the lumber camps—Del as a lumberjack and Elvera as a cook. And I've come to recognize that they and their resort provided the connective tissue that bound together our extended family, an interconnected network of uncles and aunts and cousins."

"It continues today," Glenn said. "What with an increasing crowd of nieces and nephews and grandchildren, it's more than an old man can keep track of."

The telephone was silent for a moment. Then I heard Glenn sigh before he continued. "My sister Ann taught school for all those years while she raised all those Stennes boys, they've all done so well. Then there's Claire, and Roy, and your cousin Tom—he's had a great career. And Sally, she died too early, of cancer you know."

"I know," I replied. "She came down to Minneapolis and Dad helped get her admitted to the University Hospital. I remember visiting her there. There wasn't much they could do for her back then."

"She was only sixty-four but she had a good life and a nice family," Glenn said. "Her two daughters, Carolyn and Linnea, they've done really well."

Again, I could hear a catch in Glenn's voice. "Excuse me," he said. "I get all emotional when I talk about this."

"And your mom," he continued after a moment. "She was more like a mother to me than my own mom. Hildur was always so welcoming, never judgmental. I remember one time when I was living at your house in Minneapolis. I was just out of high school, eighteen or so, and I hadn't learned to drink. I went out with a couple of my buddies and I got awfully drunk. It was really late when they dumped me on your front step. Somehow I woke up enough to flop in my bedroom. You know, behind the kitchen. In the morning Hildur shook me awake. 'I've made you lunch and some coffee,' she said. 'Maybe you'll want some before you go to work.'"

"Over breakfast she asked me if I'd learned anything. 'Yeah,' I said. She didn't say another word."

"That sounds like my mother."

"I always felt that your house was my home. And look how you kids have turned out. Your dad was great, always ready for a game of cribbage. But your mom, Hildur, was responsible for raising you. She was responsible for all the love in that house. I could feel it. We all felt that way."

"Now you've got me weeping," I said.

36

DUPONT ALLEY

I lived in the house on Dupont Avenue in south Minneapolis throughout my childhood and teenage years. I am privileged beyond measure to have nothing but fond memories of the experience—due largely to my mother's influence. I know not everyone can say the same about their childhood.

That's not to say that I appreciated everything Mom did for me. Each day during the last of the war years, Mom would line up my sisters and me at the kitchen table. "Open your mouth," she'd say, as she put two drops of cod liver oil on each of our tongues. I still harbor suspicions about the motivations behind that practice. After all, cod was the same fish they used to make lutefisk. I think they harvested the livers before they preserved the fillets—a perverse Scandinavian secret designed to torture young children. It was a plot worthy of Ingmar Bergman, the Swedish cinema director famous for making gloomy and stark movies.

Most of my memories are more pleasant.

Cod liver oil not-with-standing, mother did feed us well. Her cooking wasn't gourmet by any means, rather simple stick-to-your-ribs dishes like meatloaf, tuna casserole, and fried chicken. She often drew on the meat and eggs we got from Dad's farm in southern Minnesota—frozen beef roast, hamburger, chicken, and fresh eggs we got in thirty-dozen cartons. Her specialties were baked bread, cinnamon rolls, and donuts. And with six kids in the house, she would use shortcuts—peanut butter and jelly sandwiches on Wonder Bread, Chef Boyardee spaghetti in a can, fried Spam, and Kraft macaroni and cheese from a box.

As an admonition to clean my plate, I heard "There are children starving in China" a few times, but not with much earnestness. I do remember hiding uneaten bread crusts under the edge of my plate. She never discovered my subterfuge—at least she never called me on it. Mostly, I ate what she presented and if I didn't, I was on my own. Food was to be enjoyed but not swooned over.

As an act of contrition for poisoning me with fish oil, my mother read to me. We'd sit together on the sofa while she'd page through one of the usual array of children's books, pointing out the words. I memorized story lines before I could actually read. It's hard to admit, given current sensitivities, but one of my favorites was *Little Black Sambo*, the story of a little boy who turns a tiger into butter for his breakfast pancakes. Other favorites included the Uncle Remus stories—Br'er Rabbit, Br'er Fox, and Tar-Baby—and the Disney movie based on those stories, *Song of the South*, that Mom took me to. I know now that those stories don't register well—they promote bias and simplistic characterizations of African Americans—but, god, I did love the stories of those clever characters.

On occasion, Mom read an excerpt from one of the encyclopedia volumes that filled a couple of bookcase shelves in the sunroom, a bright and cozy space just off the living room that harbored an upright piano, a couple of arm chairs, and eventually a television set. It often served as my dad's retreat from the noise and chaos we kids created.

I remember one article Mom read from the encyclopedia about a turbaned East Indian holy man who tried not to kill anything living. He was careful not to even step on ants. I wondered how he did that and for months I tiptoed on the sidewalks, mindful of the small creatures that scurried in and out of the little mounds of sand that funneled into the cracks in the concrete.

Every so often, when I was five or six and Mom didn't want to hire a babysitter, she took me in tow to the Minneapolis Institute of Art where she would spend an hour perusing one section or another of the vast museum. I remember being mesmerized by the large Rembrandt painting of Lucretia that dominated the landing of the museum's grand staircase: a woeful look in her eye, a dagger in her hand and blood staining her white gown.

In those early years, my mother belonged to a church sewing-circle, half-a-dozen women who got together every couple of weeks to talk while they sewed or knit. As a result, we had a plethora of colorful afghan throws, each an assemblage of knitted squares, hanging over every sofa and armchair in the living room. Mom took me along, the only kid in attendance, I think because I could be relied upon to play quietly by myself for an hour or two. Maybe I was born that way, but I do remember a time when I told my mother I was bored. She responded with, "Boredom is a lack of imagination." I took her admonition to heart and ever since I've spent a lot of my life inside my head.

Mom talked the school authorities into accepting me into kindergarten a year early, when I was only four and a half. I suspect she was eager to have me out of the house so she could better attend to my younger brothers. The first day of class she walked me the few blocks to school. From then on, I was on my own. One winter morning I complained that the snow was too deep to walk to school. It was then Mom told me her story about walking two miles through the snow in long stockings pulled over her shoes. "At least you've got goulashes," she said, as she buckled my boots and pushed me out the door. I never complained again.

Mom started me on poetry when I was a toddler when she taught me her version of a common Swedish toe-naming rhyme.[29] She would hold one of my bare feet and gently squeeze my small toe between her fingers. "Little toa," she'd say. Then, moving to the next toe, "Toa tillia." Then, "Tillia rosa," Then, "Stumpa nosa." Then, as I giggled, she'd grab my big toe and give it a good pull, roll her tongue and say, "Stuuaa tumpin!" Later she read me nursery rhymes and books by Doctor Seuss (*And to Think That I Saw it on Mulberry Street* was a favorite), I memorized them all, fascinated by their clever cadence.

I took my budding interest in poetry to school. When I was in first grade my teacher had built a small stage in the corner of her classroom, a raised platform with a cardboard arch above. About once a week she invited her students to stand up there and read or do a show-and-tell. I spontaneously composed and recited poetry. My teacher wrote down what I said and gave it to my mother. It's all gone now save one first line recorded in my memory: "Have you seen my new shoes? They're made out of wood." I think the poem was inspired by a geography lesson.

With Mom's encouragement, I came to love stories—and music. In the late afternoon after school I would lay on the living room floor in front of our big counsel radio listening to the adventures of *Bring-'Em-Back-Alive Clyde Beatty*; *Sky King*; *The Green Hornet*; and *Jack Armstrong, All-American Boy*. In the evening I'd lay enraptured by the *Lone Ranger* and his sidekick Tonto—and would search through Cheerios cereal boxes for prizes or a mail-in coupon that Mom would help me fill out so I could send away for an atomic ring that (disturbingly radioactive in retrospect) glowed in the dark. Cheerios is still one of my stand-by breakfast cereals. All the story lines were simple: a virtuous hero vanquishing a bad guy and saving the community—sometimes gunplay was involved but nobody ever got killed.

As I got older, I got hooked on the resonate voice that asked "Who knows what evil lurks in the hearts of men? The Shadow knows." I got chills as the eerie creaking door introduced the *Inner Sanctum*. I was glued to the radio for *This Is Your FBI*, *Sam Spade: Private Eye*, *Suspense* and other radio theater productions. I followed *My Friend Irma*, the adventures of a new immigrant in *Life with Luigi*, and laughed at the sharp wit of Fred Allen and the characters he met on his walks down Allen's Alley, and laughed in anticipation every time Molly asked Fibber McGee to get something from their over-stuffed hall closet, chortling through the avalanche of falling objects and waiting for that delayed "clink" as the last thing fell to the floor. God, there were so many of them and they all played on my imagination, leaving me to this day with strong visual images.

I also listened in on the musical variety shows that Mom wanted to hear: *Your Hit Parade* (sponsored by Lucky Strike with the staccato prattle of an auctioneer I tried to imitate ending with, "Sold to American"); *The Bing Crosby Show* (sponsored by Chesterfield); and *Arthur Godfrey's Talent Scouts.*

When we finally got a television set, one of the last in our neighborhood, I was surprised to find out what those radio celebrities really looked like—most were just ordinary folks rather than the exotic creatures I had imagined. Back then, most songs were ballads and the music and lyrics filled my head and were hardwired into my brain. But somehow, over the years, I've found room to stuff in an appreciation for a wide variety of music—folk, jazz, rock, zydeco, klezmer, classic—you name it, but don't ask me to recall the lyrics or the artists. I can read music (I played the tuba in high school) and can sing or hum the first phrase of a lot of songs but need a score to get any further. I think Grandpa Back would not be too disappointed in my level of music appreciation.

Early television built on the popularity of radio personalities that relied on dialogue and song, but also introduced hilarious sight-gags and comedic routines that you just had to see to appreciate—some were spinoffs of old vaudeville routines. I can remember laughing hysterically at the comedic skits of Cid Cesar and Imogene Cocoa, Dean Martin and Jerry Lewis, and a host of others I got to know and love during repeated appearances on the *Colgate Comedy Hour*. And I choked with laughter at the clownish Milton Berle and giggled along with Red Skelton as he played one of his whimsical characters.

Looking back, I cherish the experience of those early days of television and the opportunity to have lived through both the years of naive innocence and to have witnessed the struggles and consternation as racial diversity was introduced on the air—breaking the color barrier, it was called—first the showcasing of established crossover stars like Louis Armstrong, Nat King Cole, and Ella Fitzgerald and progressing over decades to when, in 1968 (yes, that late) British singer Petula Clark put her hand on Harry Belafonte's arm during her television show. Yes, a lot of progress has been made since, but I don't need to be told that the struggle isn't over. As my mother would have said, "Everybody's welcome at the table, if you're willing to share."

On cold winter mornings during those postwar years I remember the smell of Lipton's chicken noodle soup wafting throughout the school building. Our teacher would serve each of us a cup of the broth first thing in the morning—a nod to good student nutrition. Hmm, hmm—cod-liver oil and Lipton's instant soup—what child could ask for greater happiness?

Before we began our school lessons, we'd all stand, put our hands over our hearts, and recite the Pledge of Allegiance to the Flag. In those days, the Pledge didn't include the phrase "under God." That was added in 1954 during the height of the scare of godless communism. Once a month, at the peak of our Russia paranoia, we would crawl under our desks as a drill in case we saw the flash of an atomic bomb explosion. I never believed my school desk, sturdy as it was, could withstand an atomic blast. I'm sure I wasn't the only kid to have occasional nightmares.

Mom introduced me to religion by enrolling me in Sunday school at Mount Olivet Lutheran Church, at the time the largest Lutheran congregation in the world. The church was under the ministerial leadership of the charismatic Reverend Reuben Youngdahl, the younger brother of Minnesota Governor Luther Youngdahl. The church was only six blocks from our house. Dad never attended church except for funerals and weddings.

For a few years I went regularly, learning all the bible stories. But one Sunday, when I was eight or nine, a young missionary was visiting from Africa. He said he went there to save the souls of the poor heathens. "If they don't hear the word of God, they're doomed to hell," he said, or words to that effect.

"Wait," I said. "You mean they're doomed if they've never even *heard* of Jesus?"

"Yes," he said.

I thought that was so blatantly unfair that I could never again put my heart into Sunday school lessons. For a couple of years after that I walked to church on Sunday mornings, but just hung around outside the church building. I walked home when the other kids were let out of class. When I got older I looked for a church that wasn't so dogmatic.

When I was old enough to be trusted not to drop the dishes, I dried while one sister washed and the other put them away, chatting away all the while. Often, one or more of my younger brothers hung around just to be part of the conversation. My mother spent those few minutes of her free time to sit by the fire or out on the screened porch to read the most recent addition of *Colliers* or *The Saturday Evening Post*. Even now, long married, I find a Zen-like spiritual satisfaction in cleaning up after a good meal.

37

CAR WARS

"Your dad just brought home another car," Mom said. "It's out in the drive."

I rushed out of the house to look. "What's this?" I asked my dad. I was a couple years short of getting my driver's permit, but my interest in cars had already peaked. Like most teenaged boys, I could distinguish one model from another at a hundred paces. Even so, this vehicle was totally unfamiliar to me.

"It's a Henry J," he said, wiping a sleek maroon-colored fender with a leather chamois. The car's white-walled tires gleamed. It was only the latest in a long string of automobiles that showed up in our drive, only to disappear a few weeks later.

Dad was a horse trader—literally. He was raised on a farm and, when he was middle-aged and established, he and his sister bought a spread down near Spring Valley, in southern Minnesota. We didn't live there but for years it was a regular source of eggs and frozen chicken. Every few weeks we'd drive down to check on the place. That's where I learned to drive a tractor, plow straight, and back a wagon.

Every so often Dad would take me to a stock auction. Before the bidding opened, we'd walk around the stables looking over horses and other livestock. Once, I was sitting next to him when a young chestnut filly was led into the bidding arena. "You interested in that one?" he asked.

"Yeah," I said. "That's the one that stepped on my foot." When the bidding was over they led the horse out of the arena. "I thought you were going to bid on her," I said.

"I did," Dad said. "She's ours."

I was dumbfounded. I never heard nor saw him bid. After that I watched for clues. It was all very subtle. When he wanted to bid he'd catch the eye of the auctioneer by raising a finger or an eyebrow. I was afraid to scratch my nose for fear of buying a steer.

We boarded the filly down at the Spring Valley farm along with a couple of other horses Dad had picked up at other auctions. He sold her a year or so later for a nice profit. He brought his horse trading skills to buying cars—you can take the boy out of the country, and all that.

Over time he brought home a rather exotic array of automobiles: the Henry J, a Nash Rambler, a Plymouth coup, a Ford Edsel, and even a squat, pigeon-toed Chevrolet Corvair, the car that Ralph Nader famously made infamous in *Unsafe at Any Speed*. But to its credit, that Corvair had a gas heater that was quick to warm on a cold Minnesota morning.

Dad would have each car checked out by a mechanic friend he helped get started in business. Then he'd give the car a good wash and vacuum and sell it, making a small profit on each one. He had to stop, or at least slow down, when he got a letter from the automobile registration office that said he must be in the used car business and would need to register his company.

It's only in hindsight that I better understand the dynamics of the automobile industry of those post-war decades. During the war years, steel was devoted to the production of war machines and the manufacture of cars came to a virtual standstill. When the war ended, the big three auto makers—General Motors, Ford, and Chrysler—immediately went back to turning out cars of pre-war design, slow to recognize the growing demand for the new and modern. Several independents—Studebaker, Hudson, Packard, Nash, and Kaiser-Frazer, among others—stepped into the breech, introducing sleeker designs and innovative engineering. Caught flat-footed, the big three retooled and introduced a broader array of models, futuristic body designs with ever more protuberant fins and bigger engines. They began to aggressively compete with the independents. By the nineteen sixties, virtually all the independent auto makers had disappeared.

And that system of streetcar trollies that I had depended on growing up, the light rail system that connected all corners of the Twin Cities (like so many other cities across the country); it was shut down in 1954. Some blamed lobbying efforts by General Motors for the system's demise, but in reality the clunky and slow old beasts succumb to buses and the proliferation of automobiles. Herbert Hoover's 1928 campaign slogan "a car in every garage" had finally come to fruition. In Minneapolis, the trolley's overhead wires came down and the rails were torn up or paved over.

In recent years, Minneapolis has tried to reclaim some of those old trolley rights-of-way for its new light rail system—the resurrection of an old concept. If you live long enough, the old becomes new again. And maybe my father should have kept some of those off-brand cars he brought home. If you can find one now, it's likely to be a rare and valuable antique.

In the years before I could drive, Dad managed ticket sales for sporting events held on the University of Minnesota campus. He always kept a few of the best seats for himself and his friends. He took me to Gopher football games, coaching me on the rules. But my favorite sport was professional basketball. The Lakers, before moving to Los Angeles, played at the university campus. We sat in the first row of the balcony where I leaned over the railing cheering all the players: the giant George Mikan, Slater Martin, Jim Pollard, and my favorite, guard Whitey Skoog. And before black players were allowed to play in any big-league sports, I was enchanted by the comedic razzle-dazzle of the Harlem Globetrotters and their ball wizardry antics as "Sweet Georgia Brown" was whistled over the loudspeakers. I knew the names of their coach and several of the players: Abe Saperstein and dribbling wizard, Marques Haynes, among others.

When I was finally old enough, I learned to drive in a Hudson Hornet, a roomy overpowered behemoth of a car that my cousin Tom and I admired as a frequent competitor at the State Fair stock car races. My favorite automobile though was a sporty light green Pontiac convertible that we all piled into late one summer for a road trip out to Glacier Park. Dad liked to drive that car home from work, the top down, wearing a jaunty cap. At a traffic stop one day he noticed a couple of young ladies gazing at the car in admiration. He was feeling a bit puffed up until he overheard one say, "Oh, he's old." Dad said he was amused by the story, but the Pontiac was gone in a week.

Dad was also a skilled handyman. Neighbors would bring him broken toasters and other small appliances that he'd fix. And when I was a teenager, I served as his helper around the house doing electrical and plumbing repairs, installing wood paneling, and painting. One summer he bought one of the now gone Quonset huts that had been erected on the University of Minnesota campus to house the onslaught of World War II veterans. He hired a couple of guys to disassemble the building and deliver all the parts to our backyard, a nail-infested hazard to be sure. I spent that summer driving nails out of the wood and sorting the boards by type and length. In addition to a pile of lumber, I had several coffee cans filled with nails of various sizes that I'd straightened and sorted at Dad's instruction. In the fall we hauled it all down to the farm and built a corncrib and a couple of chicken coops.

My ticket to teenage freedom was a used 1954 stick-shift, four-door Ford Crestline with a V-8 engine. It wasn't my car, but I had access to it more than I deserved. Throughout my teens I had a little money from various part-time jobs and a car to drive. Fortunately, I didn't have much competition from my siblings. My older sisters were usually driven around by their dates, and my younger brothers were still too young to drive. No dummy, I was always glad to run errands for my mom. What kid could ask for more?

My first real job was delivering papers. My second job was offered to me by the man who had owned the candy shop down on the corner where, when I was younger, I'd take five minutes deciding how best to spend a dime. He stopped by our house, told my mother he was going to open a small diner in the neighborhood and asked if I would work for him? Mom, not willing to answer for me, told him, "You need to talk to him yourself. He'll be home from delivering papers anytime now."

I worked at the diner until I started high school and got a job in a corner drugstore I passed on my walk home from school. There were two drugstores on that intersection, across the street from each other. Each had a soda fountain with loyal after-school clientele. It's where I met Sue

Sue and I had attended the same schools in Minneapolis—starting in grade school. She was a year behind me and I hadn't noticed her until one magical day at the drugstore. One afternoon she stepped into the store dressed in a pink shirtwaist, her dark hair and petite figure aglow, a backlit vision as she stood inside the smoke-glass door.

"Where's the pharmacy?" she asked. I was tongue-tied but managed to point to the back of the store. After she left I got her name, "Susan Shapiro," off the prescription bottle. A few days later I noticed that she walked home with a friend of mine, a guy I walked to school with every morning—we were on the ski team together. On the days I didn't have to work after school, I made a point to walk home with my friend—and with Sue.

Sue and I dated off and on throughout high school. During one of the off periods my mother asked me, "What happened to that pretty Jewish girl. I like her."

"I do too," I replied.

As I started at the University of Minnesota and Sue went off to Mills College in California, our relationship languished—until one summer when we met again back in Minneapolis. It was a sunny Sunday afternoon and we were each canoeing with our dates on one of the city lakes. We saw each other and I steered my boat alongside hers, no doubt annoying our dates by our too long and too animated conversation. That fall Sue transferred to the University of Minnesota and we were married a year later, the day after I graduated, at the First Universalist Church—by then, our church of choice.

Susan Bette Shapiro Taylor (Circa 1973)

Sue and I set up household in a little home near the university campus while she finished her senior year of college and I went to graduate school in hospital administration. As a wedding gift, Dad gave us a used Renault Dauphine, a small economy car imported from France to compete with the Volkswagen Beetle. The Renault had a rear engine that burned two quarts of oil a week. I found a source for reprocessed motor oil that sold for twenty-five cents a quart. Sue and I joked that the car ran on three cylinders and a fence post. On one cold winter day I parked the thing at a snow-covered parking lot on campus. When I came back for it after classes it wouldn't start—not even a crank. I asked a friend for a push but all four wheels where frozen in place. The car slide around the lot like a four-runner sled until we hit a patch of dry pavement and the tires caught and the engine turned over.

We hated that car and we weren't the only ones. The Renault failed to catch on in America, making several lists of the worst and dumbest cars of all time. A decade after we sold ours, the French made another attempt to enter the American market with a seductively persuasive slogan, "The Renault for people who swore they wouldn't buy another one."

I did forgive my father, it wasn't his fault..

38

FROM WIFE TO WIDOW

On January 20, 1981, the day Ronald Reagan was inaugurated President of the United States and his predecessor, Jimmy Carter, liberated the American hostages held by Iran for 444 days, I was invited to interview for a job in Karachi, Pakistan, to help commission the Aga Khan University Hospital then under construction. We would need to move to that exotic part of the world and put Jennifer and David in school there. Sue took up the idea with enthusiasm.

When I told my folks, my mother was excited about the opportunity. I wasn't so sure how my father would take the news since he was struggling with cardiac issues and late-onset diabetes. "Of course you should go," he said. "If I were you, I'd already be on the airplane."

It was only a few months later, at the end of October, that things went bad for my father. I was in the States for a business meeting with the hospital's architect in Boston. From there, I flew to Minneapolis to visit my folks. I called my Mother before I got on the airplane. "Your dad's in the hospital," she said.

It was the first I'd heard. I had a picture of what Dad was like when I last saw him and that image hadn't changed in my mind. I expected him to be just as I'd left him.

"I haven't sent you a letter yet," Mom said. And telephoning between Minneapolis and Karachi, we both knew, was problematic at best.

I went straight to my parent's house from the airport. The fall colors were past their prime. The branches of the few large elms that remained along Dupont Avenue, the grand trees that had once lined the street for miles, were skeletal. Leaves skittered in the driveway and covered the ground. There was the faint nostalgic smell in the air of someone illegally burning leaves.

Mom and I sat in the kitchen looking out at the birds perched at the edge of a large bird feeder, held at bay by a plump gray squirrel fattening up for the winter. "He doesn't leave much for the birds," I said.

Mom waited while the din of a low flying jet rattled the house. For decades we joked that the airplanes used Mom's house to line up for landing at Wold-Chamberlain Field, the Minneapolis-Saint Paul International Airport. The thundering noise and the required pause in conversation were second nature to my mother. "Even the squirrels need to eat," she said as the noise subsided.

I should have known that's what she'd say. She had watched generations of squirrels from her kitchen window. There was a nest in the hollow of an ancient oak tree that dominated the backyard. Over the years she'd seen an occasional albino poke its head out of the nest. And one year a baby that was all black. "They're all welcome," she said.

My mother looked well but worried. "Your dad's pretty sick," she said. "It's not his heart, it's colon cancer."

"Oh shit," I whispered.

As the light faded, I made a couple of Presbyterian cocktails, my mother's favorite at-home drink, and we moved into the living room so we could sit near the fireplace. She brought me up-to-date on Dad's condition and filled me in on how she was doing. She cried a little, as did I. After an hour or so she said, "It's too late to see him now. But go tomorrow. Late morning is best."

My mother met my father in 1932 at the Marigold Ballroom, a Minneapolis dance hall—a girl after her father's musical heart. She was twenty-one and working as a maid for a physician's family. He was twenty-nine, a farm boy from Buffalo Lake who worked as a storeroom clerk at the University of Minnesota. They were married by a justice of the peace at the Minneapolis Courthouse on June 9, 1935. Her sister Claire and her recently acquired husband Roy stood as witnesses.

I was born in 1940, their first boy after two girls. One of the earliest family stories that I remember was that as a baby I slept in a drawer in a trailer. When I first heard the story, my concept of a trailer was a four-sided wooden box on wheels. I imagined them putting me in a drawer, then pushing the drawer through the wall to the outside, exposed to the elements. *What if it rained?* I thought. It was a long time before I grasped the concept of a house trailer with a chest-of-drawers.

With a growing family, my folks moved to a small home on Aldridge and 53rd Street South, then the southern edge of Minneapolis. I only have a few memories of living there. One was the iceman who came by every day or so to push a block of ice through a small door in the outside wall into our icebox. Another was the neighbor's horse team running through our backyard, and every backyard down the block, leaving torn-up flower beds and broken picket fences in its wake. The last image I have is viewing my newborn brother, Steve, snug in a wicker basket inside the home's front entrance. The next thing I knew we had moved to a larger house on Dupont Avenue South, where my parents still lived.

Late the next morning, as Mom suggested, I stopped by my father's hospital room. As I poked my head in, an attending nurse said, "I'm done here. He's all yours."

Dad was in an observation ward with a glass wall to the nursing station and monitors pulsing above his head. An intravenous drip was stuck in his good arm. He was lying on his side, awake, but looking at the wall. "Who is it?" he asked with a weak voice.

"It's me, Bob, your number-one son."

I heard a quiet gasp and saw his shoulders shake. With some effort he rolled over on his back, looked at me and smiled. "Thanks for coming," he said. "I'm glad you're here."

For ten minutes, with determination that surprised me, he brushed off my questions and peppered me with his own about Pakistan and my new job: "How do you like it there? How's Sue? Tell her thanks for the letters. How are the kids doing? Are they treating you right at work?"

After the basics were covered, we settled into reminiscing about our lives together as father and son.

"I remember a time we were driving down to Spring Valley, to the farm, just you and me," I said. "We stopped at a cheese store and you asked the salesman if the limburger cheese was ripe. I remember his drawl, 'Mister, ain't nothing more gonna happen to that cheese.' You bought a big chunk and the car stunk for a month. Mom thought something died in there."

Dad nodded his head. "Maybe it was the same trip," he said. "You were twelve or thirteen, painting the chicken coup, and you told me you knew why I wanted you to go to school."

"How could I forget?" I said. "It was a hundred degrees in the shade and you were abusing the child labor laws."

"Do you remember the first time you took me pheasant hunting out at Buffalo Lake?"

"Yes," he said. "I let you use a single shot .22 loaded with BB shot. You got a bird as I remember."

"I thought I was big stuff. I also remember you telling me about growing up out there. You said that one fall you and your older brother put empty crockery jugs in the bottom of the silo, before your dad loaded in the corn mash for feeding the stock. The next summer those jugs were filled with alcohol that had seeped through the sides. Your brother was called Ki, for whiskey, and you were called Little-Ki."

"The stuff was probably poisonous," Dad said. "We weren't as well behaved as you were. When I was a teenager our outhouse got tipped over more than one Halloween, so one year my brother and I moved the outhouse back about four feet. We had to move it back in place before dad got up in the morning to take a leak and there was evidence that someone had an unpleasant surprise. No one ever tipped over our outhouse again!"

"I remember your dad, Grandpa Albert," I said, "but just a little. I remember him teaching me how to feed a squirrel. It was at his place in northeast Minneapolis. He said the trick was to get them to come to you. It was a good lesson for a lot of things in life."

"He was a wise buzzard," Dad said. "When we lived on the farm he raised cattle. When my brother Earl took over, he started raising sheep. Dad called them 'god-damn-sheep,' all one word."

"I remember one summer driving out to Buffalo Lake with Grandpa. This was before seatbelts. He stopped the car suddenly and I put a spider-web crack in his windshield with my head."

"That explains a lot," Dad quipped.

"Very funny," I said. "When I got to the farm I was assigned the responsibility of feeding a baby lamb whose mother had died. It would suck so hard it about yanked the milk bottle out of my hands. Then it followed me around everywhere like I was its momma."

"He was teaching you a lesson in responsibility, I think."

Dad liked a good joke and he was a kind-hearted and principled man. But he was taciturn. At times I'm not much different, a product of the stoic gene-pool from which I emerged.

I remembered one time when Grandma Back was visiting. While Dad read the newspaper, she peppered him with questions about world events. She became increasingly annoyed by his lack of attention until finally, after he'd finished his reading, he set down the paper and proceeded to answer each of her questions in turn. She was determined to have a conversation with him. It was one of her favorite stories she told about him over the years. "It was so Glen," she said.

But that morning in the hospital, Dad and I had a better conversation than I think we'd ever had, except about hospital management, our shared profession. We laughed and cried together until I could tell he was too tired to continue.

"See you tomorrow," I said, but I think he was already asleep.

The next morning I went back to pick up where we left off. After an hour of more reminiscing, I said, "I'm scheduled to leave early tomorrow, but I think I should stay."

He was emphatic. "No. You've got a job and family waiting for you and a life to lead. Get on with it."

Without thinking much about it, I blurted out a question that I had been reluctant to ask, it seemed so final, "Did I ever thank you for being a great dad?"

"Yes," he said, "a few times, one way or another. You've been a good son."

"I love you," I said, and kissed him on his forehead.

"I love you too," he responded. I knew he did, but I think it was the first time I'd heard him say so.

My father died less than a week later at the age of seventy-nine. He and my mother had been married forty-six years.

39

HERE AND NOW AND FAR AWAY

A year after my father's death, Sue and I invited my mother to visit us for Christmas in Karachi. She flew over with a couple she knew from Bemidji, the parents of a young woman we'd met who was married to a successful Pakistani businessman.

Mom arrived with a big suitcase full of presents and a small suitcase full of clothes. Among the presents was a bag of avocados which we immediately made into guacamole. The rest we placed under the heavily decorated branches of our plastic tree to await Christmas Eve.

We kept Mom busy, taking her to a Christmas concert held at the Holy Trinity Cathedral and a Christmas gala at the gaily decorated American Counsel General's residence. Christmas Eve day we were again invited over to the Counsel General's home, along with all the kids from the Karachi American School and their parents. Two donkeys were tied up in the yard, along with a camel. A small flock of lambs milled about inside a fenced pen. A skinny Santa Claus, bearded and sweating in his traditional red fur-trimmed suit, arrived in a white Victoria carriage pulled by two white horses. He tossed handfuls of Tootsie Rolls and Tootsie Pops to the screaming throng of children. I nabbed one of each.

That night, after a quiet evening opening presents around our tree, we drove to a nearby Jesuit monastery where we heard they were going to stage an outdoor Christmas pageant. The monastery was located on a wooded estate at the edge of the city. We followed directions to an unmarked entrance and turned onto a narrow gravel roadway that curved through a stand of trees hiding the buildings beyond. Several cars were already in the parking lot and others were arriving behind us.

Kerosene torches provided dim yellow light as we found our way to wooden benches set in a semicircle. The night air smelled of straw and animals and the ever-present hint of burning charcoal. It was surprisingly cold and we shivered in spite of our Minnesota sweaters and wool socks.

"Who would'a thought it could get this cold in Karachi?" I said, my hands deep in my pockets.

"I wish I'd brought my long underwear," Sue added.

"Mom, are you warm enough?" I asked.

"Just fine," she said, her Minnesota constitution impervious to anything short of thirty-below-zero.

Inside the circle of chairs a menagerie of donkeys, goats, and sheep was assembled among bales of hay that surrounded a canvas tarp suspended on four wooden poles. An illuminated white parchment star hung above.

I looked at the star. *The one on our house is bigger,* I thought.

That uncharitable reflection was immediately followed by a memory of my mother saying, *'Robert James Bobby Jim, count yourself again.'* It was a chastisement she gave me as a child when I puffed myself up. "There's only one of you," she'd said. "You don't count for more than anyone else."

Anything else you want to complain about? I asked myself. "My feet are cold," I said.

After the crowd settled, an amplified voice began to recite the Christmas story from Luke. "In those days Caesar Augustus issued a decree that a census should be taken of the entire Roman world. And everyone went to his own town to register…" As the voice read, a young Joseph in turban and smock led a donkey toward the tent with the expectant Mary, dressed in blue, riding on its back.

The couple settled under the tent and the lights dimmed while the star glowed brightly. Off to the side two shepherds with long staffs pointed at the star as a half dozen lambs milled about at their feet.

The voice read, "And there were shepherds living in the fields nearby, keeping watch over their flocks at night." A horn trumpeted as the voice said, "An angel of the Lord appeared to them… and suddenly a great company of the heavenly host appeared with the angel, praising God."

The lights on the manger came back up as three wise men leading live camels walked in from the wings to pay homage to the newborn. The disembodied voice faded and the assemblage settled into the scene, forming a life-sized crèche as a recording of the *Halleluiah Chorus* began playing over the loud speakers.

We walked back to the car, stomping our numb feet and slapping ourselves with unmittened hands to regain circulation in our cold limbs. Mom slipped her hand under my arm. "I remember when I was a child," she said, "We had a Christmas pageant at our school. I remember there were candles on the tree. It was magical. Thank you for bringing me."

When we got home to our unheated house, we sat in the kitchen around the open oven door warming our hands. That night we all slept under heavy blankets, visions of sugar plums dancing in our heads.

The day after Christmas the five of us flew to Bombay (now Mumbai), the start of a two-week tour of India. Mid-morning, driving from the airport to our hotel, we passed miles of squatters living along the road's margins—adults and children hunkering in the shade of canvas lean-tos and dented sheet metal, or lying on string cots, *charpois*, hemmed in on all sides by rushing traffic. "How desperate," Mom said. "How sad."

When we arrived at the Taj Mahal hotel we were struck by its overdone palatial façade, an uncomfortable contrast to the desolate squatters. In the lobby Mom looked around at all the opulent luxury. "What a privilege to be here," she said, putting things in perspective. "We *must* enjoy ourselves," she added, as if it was an obligation.

As obedient children, we tried to do our duty.

After a day of touring we decided to dine in the hotel's fine restaurant. We were escorted to our table by a tall, turbaned Sikh, his black beard cradled in a black silk Jaali. Mother followed in his wake as if she were the Queen of England. "This is nice," she said as we settled in. "Do you think they can make a Manhattan?"

"Let's see," I offered, as our tuxedoed waiter approached. "Can you make a Manhattan?"

"I will check, sir," said the waiter. When he returned he said, "The bartender says we have sweet vermouth but not American whiskey."

"Tell him to use brandy," I suggested. "And please ask him to be sure to put in a Maraschino cherry and some of the juice. Make it three, please."

The waiter returned and swept a tray of drinks unto the corner of the table, three generous highballs and glasses of soda for Jennifer and David.

"Here's to a great trip," I said, as we all took sips from our drinks.

Mom looked admiringly at the glass in her hand. "This is the best Manhattan I've ever had."

We flew on to Udaipur where we boated to the filigreed Lake Palace, a magical vision of white marble floating in the middle of Lake Pichole. A sari-clad woman greeted each of us as we disembarked, pressing her painted finger to our foreheads and adorning our necks with leis of marigolds. The next day we toured the ancient sites, bought patinated silver necklaces and clunky bracelets fashioned in the style of Indian tribal nomads. We bumped and rattled our way back to our hotel boat-launch on the thinly cushioned bed of a two-wheeled tonga.

After a nap we went to dinner. "I really enjoyed the day," my mother said, as we settled at our table.

Sue and I were impressed with how well she'd stood up at the bazaar, climbing endless steps, and enduring the rough tonga ride.

"Do you think they can make a Manhattan?" Mother asked, a pattern emerging. Her at-home drink was a Presbyterian—a shot of bourbon drowned in a mix of club soda and ginger ale. A Manhattan was for a special night on the town.

We went through the now familiar routine with our waiter. This time the bartender could only offer Scotch as an alternative to bourbon or brandy—a Rob Roy, actually. No matter. After a couple of sips my mother looked at her glass and said with a twinkle in her eye, "This is the best Manhattan I've ever had."

From Udaipur, our daughter Jennifer flew back to Karachi to spend New Year's with her boyfriend, while the rest of us flew on to Jaipur and the Rambagh Palace.

In the morning light we drank coffee on the hotel's terrace, admiring the expansive lawns—invitingly green and rimmed by flowers in reds and yellows. A small group of women dressed in orange and saffron saris sat on the grass nearby smoking *charas*, hashish, and threading flowers in long garlands for that evening's New Year's festivities. It was easy to imagine ourselves as haughty British colonialists at the height of the Raj, sitting in these same lush gardens, sipping tea and feeling entitled. I felt thrilled and, as my mother's boy, privileged.

Like good tourists, we spent the day visiting forts and palaces and historic oddities—and rode an elephant. "That was fun," my mother enthused. "I've never ridden an elephant before."

In the evening we ate and partied under tents on the palace lawn, sipping the best Manhattans any of us had ever had. Sue and I won a dance contest as we welcomed in the New Year, 1983.

From Jaipur I hired a car and driver and we drove east to Agra, a longer trip than we expected—me riding up front in the suicide seat and none of us with seat belts. In those days the road was a narrow two-lane ribbon that cut through a smattering of small towns that stretched through one of Rajasthan's fertile valleys. The road was heavily traveled and our driver was constantly beeping his horn as we passed horse-drawn carts and motorbikes or hugging the shoulder as heavily loaded trucks careened by.

We were still an hour from Agra when daylight began to fade. In the dimming haze we drove slowly through a small village where simple homes of concrete block and red clay tile pinched the highway. Large acacia trees lined our path, their overhanging branches and white painted trunks forming a cloistering tunnel. Within feet of our car women tended cooking fires, the smoke an ethereal mist in our headlights and the aroma of charcoal prickling our nostrils. "This is *so* India," I said, more to myself than anyone.

My reverie turned to terror as the road opened on the other side of town, a palpable anxiety we all shared. The traffic moved faster. Oncoming traffic emerged from the now murky black into the dim glow of our headlights. We seemed to be the only vehicle with our headlights on. As trucks roared out of the dark and rumbled by I could feel hands pressing against the back of my seat while I created craters in the dashboard and floor. I was thankful our driver was moving slowly and maintaining a cautious intimacy with the shoulder of the road. Even so, by the time we reached our hotel at Agra we were all wrecked.

That evening over a round of drinks Mom said, "That was an exciting drive." She picked up her near empty glass. "That was the best Manhattan I've ever had."

"Por toppen?" she added. It meant 'a little on top' and was one of the few Swedish phrases she used with any regularity. "Do you think we might have another?"

"Most certainly," I said. Sue and I joined her.

The next day we visited the Taj Mahal, lingering into the evening to see that magnificent shrine to love glowing in the light of the moon. From Agra we drove onward to New Delhi where David and I flew back to Karachi. Sue and Mom stayed on a couple of days to bark at the New Delhi moon.

One cloudless day after the women got back to Karachi we took Mom out to French Beach, a secluded retreat a few miles outside the city. Along with another expatriate family, we rented a small concrete block hut from a local Baluchi fishing village. With its dirt floor, open holes for windows, and a door that kept out only things that didn't want to get in, our hut was as charming as a Tijuana jail. A water wallah, wearing a large metal funnel as a hat, led his barrel-burdened camel from hut to hut filling our latrine roof tanks with sea water. Our retreat's only saving grace was its view of a small aqua-colored cove with access to a beach of fine sand.

Mom seemed right at home in the simplicity and grandeur of the place. "No electricity, no telephone, this is wonderful. It reminds me of the homestead," she said. In the late afternoon she stood with me at the water's edge, our bare toes mingling with the sand. "You're living pretty well," she said.

Two weeks later Mom flew back to Minnesota. At the Karachi airport she said, "Thank you for a lovely visit," and gave me a hug.

I hugged her back. "You're the best mom I've ever had," I whispered, and waved her goodbye.

40

ROCKY MOUNTAIN HIGH

"This is really exciting," Mother said, as we stepped forward in the line to board the gondola at Vail. As we clambered in, we were each given a shot of Schnapps in a small plastic cup. It was mid-September, 1987, and we were going up the mountain to enjoy dinner and music, part of Vail's annual fall festival.

As we started our assent, the gondola still swinging gently, Mom offered a toast. "Here's to us and a beautiful fall." We all raised our cups. This was going to be a spectacular conclusion to a perfect mountain day.

When we finished our tour in Pakistan, Sue and I and our son David moved to Colorado, renting a house in East Vail. Jennifer was at college out east. What kept us sane in Karachi was our hope to live in the mountains when it was over, although I was a little soft on what exactly I was going to do for a living when we got there. I didn't want to return to a normal job in hospital administration, even though I had always enjoyed the work. I'd been there, done that, and wanted something challenging and new. Talk about arrogance and Pollyanna optimism!

Out of the ether, I got a call from a fellow I'd worked with in Karachi. He had recently left his position at the Secretariat, the Aga Khan's administrative offices at his Aiglimont estate just outside Paris.

"I've got a job in Jakarta, Indonesia," he said, "and I need some help. You interested?"

That was the start of Sue and my careers as international consultants. We bought a house in Edwards, at 7,200 feet elevation, a few miles down-valley and west of Vail, and invited my mother out for a visit.

We spent a couple of days with my mother driving back roads, gasping at the sweep of golden aspen reaching down from the high sugared peaks like yellow cotton blankets glowing iridescent in the sun, shamelessly garish against dappled white snow and green conifers. The high mountain meadows were a dizzying mix of reds and countless shades of amber. Yellow cottonwoods lined the rivers and streams with red scrub-oak and mountain mahogany climbing their banks.

"I've always loved fall," Mom said. "When I was young, I so enjoyed walking through the woods. And in Minneapolis I loved the smell of burning leaves. First your dad, then you boys would rake the leaves into the street and light them afire."

"We had to jump in them first," I said. "*Then* we'd burn them. You can't do that anymore. I understand why, but I miss the smell, too."

"But I've never seen a fall like this," Mom said. "All the color is up where you can see it. It just glows."

Riding the gondola up the mountain as the day faded to dusk, we watched the yellow aspen passing beneath us, giving way to lodgepole pine as we ascended. Near the summit a light snow began to fall, large flakes dancing in the air. By the end of the evening, four or five inches of snow had already fallen, with more underway.

As we descended, our gondola gently swaying, we were mesmerized as the twinkling lights of Vail's fairytale village emerged through a lacy curtain of snow. "It's just magical," Mom said. "How lucky I am. I've had a wonderful fall and now winter, all in the same day."

It wasn't long after that visit that Mom began to falter. She was still living alone in the big house on Dupont Avenue, but her memory lapses were becoming more frequent. Over the next few years she became increasingly forgetful, a little uncertain what she was supposed to do next. Gail felt Mom should no longer drive or go grocery shopping alone. She also worried that Mom might hurt herself living alone.

It was only a few months after Mom came to visit us that spring in Washington, DC, that Gail called to say, "We need to get somebody to live with her."

My brother Steve moved in for several months but it became clear Mom needed more than just a companion. It was less than a year until we had to place her in a nursing home.

41

MOTHER'S WIT AND WISDOM

I was still upset after Sue and I strolled with Mom in the garden at the nursing home and she had asked the question, "Who are you?" Throughout lunch Mom was pleasant but still vague on who we were. "We need to talk with my brothers and sisters," I told Sue. "I wonder how they're coping with all this."

That evening we sat down with Gail and her daughter, Marta, at Gail's home. Marta set out a plate of cookies and poured each of us a glass of wine.

"Yes, Mom's slipping," Gail said.

"It's hard to see day-to-day," Marta offered, "but it's pretty obvious when I look back on how she was even a couple of years ago. It's not just her mental capacity, it's physical too. She's getting weaker and less and less able to do things. But she's always had such a good sense of humor, at least until recently. I remember taking her out for a ride around Lake Harriet. 'Oh good,' Grandma said. 'I love going hither and thither.' On the ride I went around a curve a little too fast and Grandma was thrown against the door. When we straightened out, she leaned over to me and said, 'That was a little more thither than I expected.'"

"It was cloudy and cold," Marta continued, "but we stopped at the Lake Harriet pavilion and got popcorn and sat on a bench looking out at the lake. 'Do you do this often?' Grandma asked. 'What?' I responded. 'Sit out in the cold eating popcorn? No, I've never done

• 201

this before,' I said. 'I've never done this before either,' she said."

Gail took a sip of wine, sat back and cupped her fingers around the glass. "There are so many funny stories. Sad, I suppose, but funny, or poignant. Marta and I started recording them in this book." She picked up a fabric-covered notebook with a label on the cover, *Hildur's Book*. "Let me read you a few."

"Mom was always appreciative and she said things like, 'You're so good to me. And I'm so old to you.' After having her teeth cleaned she said, 'Well, I guess I can't chew tobacco for a while.' One time when Marta was visiting she said, 'I'd like to find a lover.' Marta asked, 'What kind of lover do you want?' 'Oh, I don't know. A cat, maybe.'"

"Here's another," Gail continued. "Mom always wanted to have something to do. In spite of her disabilities, she still wanted to be useful. At one time she said to Marta, 'I think I have a job.' Marta asked, 'Oh, what kind of job is it?' Hildur replied, 'I think I blow up balloons.'"

"On another occasion she said, 'I have a job.' Again, 'What kind of job is it?' 'I'm not sure,' said Mom. 'And I don't think I'm very good at it. But it's good to have work.'"

"When asked what she'd like to eat, she replied, 'Oh, I like anything and everything, but not too much of either one.' On a similar occasion when a tray was held out to her, she said, 'Oh, this and that,' and after a slight pause, 'and something else, too.'"

"When I'd go to visit she might ask, 'Why did you come?'"

"'Because I missed you,' I responded."

"'Well, who was I?'"

"One last one," Gail said. "Mom likes to compliment people. Once she looked at me and said, 'You look really nice.' I thanked her and she looked at me expectantly for a moment, and then said, 'Well?'"

As Gail continued paging through the book, I said, "Mom didn't remember who I was today, or Sue. Does she remember you or anybody in the family?"

"No, not really anymore. But here's a note from a year ago or so when her memory would fade in and out. One time she asked, 'Was I married?'"

"Yes," I said. "You were married"

"'Oh, what was my husband's name?'"

"Glen," I offered, but she showed no recognition. "Glen," I repeated. "Glen Taylor." Still no recognition. But after a pause she said, 'Glen Taylor. Oh, I loved him.'"

"You had six children," I said. 'Oh!' she said, 'I wouldn't do anything like that.'"

Yes, She Would!
Sandy, Bert, Gail, Bob, Dave, Steve (2000)

"Those are priceless," Sue said, wiping tears from her eyes. I wasn't sure if she had been laughing or crying, maybe both.

I was feeling guilty and thinking how much we had missed, living so far away. Mom had slipped away in bits and pieces, even as her core self—a loving and witty woman—had endured well after her memory had faded.

"She was a wise woman," I said. "I remember when we were kids. Mom would get up an hour before the rest of us, make a pot of coffee, and sit down to read the paper. She said she liked to ease into the day. I've tried to follow her example. I'd rather get up early than start the morning in a rush."

"Me too," Gail said. "I remember that she loved to sleep out on the screened porch, loved the sounds of the crickets and the smell of the night air."

"She'd sleep out there well into the fall," I said, "all wrapped up in a comforter."

"She was an outdoor girl," Gail added. "I think she got that from living in the north woods when she was a child,"

"Mary Sue told me a story," I said, (she had been married to my brother, David). "She was staying with Mom for several weeks while David was away at military boot camp. One day, a couple of weeks into her stay, she was sitting at the breakfast table with Mom, pouting and feeling lonely. 'I can't stand this waiting,' she said. Mom patted her hand and said, 'Don't wish away any day.'"

"What I loved most about Hildur was her inclusiveness," Sue said. "She was so welcoming and loving. From the beginning, even before we were married, I always felt part of the family."

"Another story," said Marta. "I was in the car with Grandma. We were in the backseat, driving up to Bemidji. I was knitting a sweater, needles clicking and chatting away, being my usual self. Grandma leaned over and said, 'Can't you just do nothing and enjoy the scenery?'"

"Learn to do nothing," I repeated. "There's a skill worth having."

"You've learned your lesson well," Sue snickered.

"I practice every morning," I said. "I start each day with a cup of coffee and stare into space for half an hour. I like to think of it as a spiritual practice."

"I believe Mom was a very spiritual person," Gail said. "She went to church, sure, but it was more than that."

"She always had a calm presence about her," I added. "She'd really focus on the task at hand or whomever she was with. She'd give you her full attention. Maybe that's why everyone of us kids think we're her favorite."

42

CELEBRATION OF LIFE

"Mom's failing," Gail said over the telephone. "I don't think she's got long."

"Oh dear," I whispered. "Is there anything you want me to do?"

"Call Jennifer and David," she said. "We've got everybody else covered."

"I think we can get a flight into Minneapolis tomorrow."

"Good," Gail said. "I need some help with this."

Sue and I met Gail at the nursing home. It was late September of the year 2000, and a large display of fall colors—orange pumpkins, green gourds, and sprigs of red and yellow maple leaves—adorned a round table in the lobby.

"I should warn you," Gail said. "She's unconscious and doesn't look very good."

We walked to the elevator, passing through a gauntlet of residents in wheelchairs. I smiled benignly, but I could see my own sorrow and resignation mirrored in their pleading eyes. One woman lifted her head and whispered conspiratorially, "Take me home."

"I'm sorry," I said, swallowing my guilt and averting my eyes as we continued to the elevator.

As the elevator door opened I could smell the faint aroma of disinfectant. I was thankful that the staff was so conscientious in keeping the place and the residents clean and orderly. Gail had done a good job of selecting the place and it eased my guilt, at least a bit, for being so distant and uninvolved in Mom's care.

My first impression when I saw Mom lying in her bed was how old and small she had become—her eyes were closed, her mouth was open and her breath labored. Her gaunt cheeks were withdrawn and her skull was barely contained by the sallow parchment skin of her face. I took her boney hand in mine. Her skin was cool. She gave no response.

"She's been like this for several days," Gail said. "I don't know how long she can hold on."

"They say that hearing is the last to go," Gail said as she moved to Mom's bedside and picked up her hand. "Mother? It's me Gail. Bob and Sue are here, too. Everybody is here or will arrive today. We're planning to gather here at the nursing home tomorrow. We've reserved a nice room downstairs. It's ours for the day. We've got a caterer bringing plenty of food."

We moved away from the bed. "Do you think she'll last that long?" I asked.

"I don't know. If she doesn't, we'll hold a celebration of her life in the chapel."

"If everyone will be here," offered Sue, "maybe we should hold a celebration regardless."

Gail and I both nodded our heads. "Good idea," Gail said. "We can talk to the chaplain, Reverend Hausske. He's a nice man and knows Mom pretty well."

As we stepped into the hallway just outside Mom's room, Gail said, "I've been in contact with the funeral parlor so they're prepared. But I need your help picking out a casket. I am not up to doing that alone. We can go there now if you're ready."

"Yes, let's," I said. "Do you want to come along?" I asked Sue.

"No, this is something you two need to do together. I'll stay with Hildur for a while. I'll meet you back at Gail's place."

Gail and I had no trouble agreeing on a simple casket in natural oak. It seemed in keeping with Mom's fondness for nature and the out-of-doors.

Even in her dying, my mother had a lesson for us on how to live. Given her genes, she died young, a month short of her ninetieth birthday. Her body was wasted away from a prolonged fight with Alzheimer's. Yet her spirit was full of grace and her family and friends hovered around her like a heavenly multitude.

Mid-afternoon the next day, about fifty of us gathered in the chapel to celebrate her life. We each took our turn and, with cracked and quavering voices, told our personal stories of how this simple but remarkable woman had added special meaning to our lives. Some stories were filled with wit and humor, some poignant, some grounded in solid motherly advice, and some—because not everyone is articulate at such times—an incoherent babble of sobs and non-sequiturs.

Our shared affection and respect for Hildur Florence Back Taylor filled the room. As I listened to the dozens of personal accounts, I could not help but feel that each person there might well have said, "Hildur loved me best." Apparently it wasn't just her children.

I was particularly amused by an account told by one of Mom's granddaughters, Britt Melby: "When I was living with Grandma I worked downtown and would usually take the bus and leave my car at Grandma's house, a sporty Pontiac Thunderbird. One morning she asked, 'Can I use your car today?'

"I said, sure, what are you going to do with it? She said, 'I want to go to the grocery store. The bag boys think it's such a cool car for a grandmother to drive.'"

Mary Sue, my brother David's former wife, but still very much a part of the family, captured the essence of all that was being said. "She gave us love and spirit and joy, but most of all she gave us each other. She helped us know each other, to share each other's lives. Her spirit connects us all."

The testimonials went on for well over an hour. And then we ate.

A spread of salads, cheeses, meats, and breads, with a few bottles of inexpensive wine, and, of course, desserts and coffee had been set out on a long table draped to the floor with a white cotton table cloth. Simple fare, but we Minnesotans are better at talking when we are feeding and drinking. More stories were told, some too irreverent, racy, or bold to have been offered in the chapel. Some stories were stimulated by the accounts of others, and some encouraged by the wine.

I pulled aside my sister Sandra. "What was it like for you?" I asked. For several years she had lived in a two story prairie style house that backed up to my Mom's next-door-neighbor.

"You remember that my kids often went to visit their grandma," Sandy began. "They'd zip out our back door and slip through a gap in the back fence. Next thing I knew, they were eating cookies at Mom's. I never worried about them."

Sandy paused before continuing. "I miss Mom. I used to walk over to her place myself. We'd sit on the back porch and sip tea or coffee. Maybe we'd talk or we'd just sit quietly and read. Sometimes we'd bake cookies together or sort through blueberries and bake pies. It was easy being with her. I've missed that over these last few years. She hasn't recognized me for a long time. It's been painful to be with her."

After an hour or so, as the food and drink thinned, guests began to wander back to Hildur's room. She had lain in bed for ten days without eating, taking a little water, but mostly sleeping and seemingly unaware. Her room had been filled, day and night, with family and friends sitting vigil. While she had shown no signs of awareness, her room had been overflowing with sound and activity: people talking to her, people talking about her, nurses, therapists, and aides providing medications, changing her linens, giving her baths and massage, and chaplains leading prayers and reading favorite Bible texts. All the while CDs, provided by the music therapist, played softly in the background.

Now, with everyone fed, the ceremony celebrating her life concluded, many of us crowded into her room to say our last goodbyes. With the throng assembled, Mother grabbed my brother Steve's hand and opened her eyes. She looked past him to some unknown time or place, took a final rasping breath, and died.

Mom had made the most of the moment. Always considerate, she had politely waited until we had all freed ourselves from work and obligations, made our travel plans, arrived at her side, said our piece, and had a little something to eat and drink. As so often in her life, she made a gift of her dying. She gave us the time to grieve, to celebrate, and to say goodbye. It seems she wanted to stay around long enough for us to gather near, to reconnect with each other as much as with her. No doubt she also wanted us to hear all the good stories people had to tell about her. But, as always, it was more for us than her.

Such grace.

43

FOUND

My Aunt Claire died in 2007, a month after turning one hundred, sharp until the end. Aunt Ann, age ninety-eight, followed Claire by a couple of weeks, checking herself into the hospital with chest pains after a day of running errands for elderly shut-ins.

Uncle Glenn died in 2015, at ninety-one, the last of the six Back children. On the flight into Tucson to attend his celebration, I lost my hearing aids—I'm getting old now, too. The details of what was said at the service are a bit hazy.

The memorial was held at an old mission church on the edge of town. While nice things were being said about him, I was in my head, thinking about how much I cherished his love when I was a kid and how relieved I was to have recorded at least a few of the rich stories that he and his sisters had offered.

As a Marine color-guard draped a flag over Glenn's coffin, I realized I had never asked him about his years in the service. I was also painfully aware that when I had interviewed him, as well as Claire and Ann, I had not known enough to ask all the right questions. There were so many gaps in my knowledge and understanding that I could no longer fill. I had at least a dozen mini-tapes at home, half of which I had transcribed. I vowed I'd review them all again to refresh my memory of all that I had heard.

After the service, I gave my condolences to Glenn's wife, Marilyn.

"I am so glad you came," she said. "Glenn was so fond of you."

"He was my favorite uncle."

"You know he searched high and low for that tape of your mother's. He looked everywhere."

"I'm sorry I put him through all that."

"Oh, don't be sorry. He wanted to find it as much as you did. Maybe it will turn up when I move. I want to downsize, someplace closer to our son, Peter."

"Well, if the tape shows up, great. But please don't put yourself out. You've put in enough effort already."

When I got back home my good intensions to review the tapes and get back to writing were sidetracked by a bad case of writer's block—I did not know how to compile the folktales I had accumulated into any kind of compelling narrative. I was confident that I knew the truth of the stories, but too many of the details were missing. I could compose a litany of events from what I'd heard, but I'd need to create scenes and make up lost conversations to bring the stories to life. Did that break the barrier between nonfiction and fiction? Was a writer permitted to do that?

I voiced my frustration to my writing instructor, an author of several historical books about south Florida. "You're permitted a good deal of leeway with folktales," he said. "You just need to respect the truth and steer clear of glorification or exaggeration."

"Thanks, that helps."

"Another thing," he added. "Remember, it's your story too. Put yourself in the narrative. It's another memoir."

The idea that it was a memoir had never occurred to me. The concept opened some attractive options. *I can do that,* I thought.

I made some notes, but I still didn't get back to the work of writing. I had lots of excuses. I had recently finished another memoir, *Hardship Post*, an account of our years in Pakistan, and I was not yet ready to devote the psychic energy and intense effort required for another book. In addition, Sue and I were giving serious consideration to moving from Florida to Colorado. This new book on my family heritage would need to wait, yet again.

"We can get rid of that," Sue said, "and that."

We were in the garage of our Florida home, sorting pieces of copper and brass we had accumulated when we lived in Pakistan. There were seventy or eighty pieces laid out on top of and under a makeshift of folding tables and upturned boxes.

"What were we thinking?" Sue said.

"I think you were considering going into the import business."

"That must be it," she said. "But I confess that I'm fond of a lot of this stuff. It brings back good memories."

"Yes, it does."

"But we've had it all for over thirty years," she continued. "Most of it has been in boxes all that time. There won't be room in our new place, and it would cost a lot to ship it to Colorado."

"I know, I know," I said.

"What about this piece?" she asked, picking up a wood and brass flare gun salvaged from one of the ships driven up on a Pakistani beach.

"That is so neat," I said.

"You're not helping," Sue said. "It's heavy and probably worth something. I'm sure the auction house would love to have it."

"And the ship's telegraph, too, I suppose?" The telegraph stood four feet tall and had a bell that dinged as you cranked the brass handle around its glass-faced display. It had been salvaged from a Portuguese ship and had stood sentry by the front door of every place we'd lived for the last three decades.

Sue looked at me, not saying a word, waiting for me to process my thoughts.

"It's really heavy and bulky and probably wouldn't survive the trip," I said. "And Colorado's a thousand miles from any ocean." I paused and scratched my nose. "I saw one at the marine store. They were asking over a thousand dollars for it. I guess it needs to go."

"Good," Sue said, as we continued the culling process.

"You know, I've said I'd never move again," Sue mused. "We've gotten rid of stuff every time. David's house looks like our place use to, and Jennifer has her own look. We've had garage sales and taken load after load to Goodwill, and still we've got too much stuff. Now here we are, at it again. I really want to move to Colorado, but this is the last time we do this."

"This is the nineteenth time we've moved in our fifty-five years of marriage," I said. "And you've said the same thing after every move. We're pathologically unsettled."

"The last time," Sue declared.

An auction house in Sarasota sent a van to pick up most of the brass and copper. We set aside a few pieces we just couldn't part with and sold the rest at a neighborhood rummage sale along with a too-big-to-travel BBQ smoker, a garden rake with a loose handle, and other items once cherished but now overused or out-of-favor. We left a couple pieces of furniture with a consignment shop and deposited several boxes of stuff at Goodwill.

I called the local public radio station and told them we wanted to donate our 1994 Toyota Camry. We'd bought the car new and it had 194,000 miles on it. I had ambitions to drive it until it had 200,000, but there wasn't time before we moved, and I was not sure it would survive the trip to Colorado.

"We'll send a truck to pick it up on Thursday, early afternoon," they said.

Thursday morning I was sorting books and papers in my office, filling empty liquor boxes with books I thought our local bookstore might like. Those they didn't, I'd donate to the public library. I was also packing notebooks and papers for my writing project into cardboard cartons. I pulled out a shoebox where I'd stored the mini-cassettes I'd used to interview my relatives. Behind it was another small box I didn't recognize. "What's in here?" I mumbled.

The box contained an old pair of earphones, a few photo slides of a years-ago presentation, and one unlabeled full-sized cassette—not a mini like the others.

"What's this?" I said, as I turned the cassette over in my hands. "Could it be? I wish I had a way to play it." I had given away my cassette player years ago.

Wait! There's a cassette player in the Camry. Will it still work? I hadn't used it in years. I looked at my watch. It was near noon. *They could come any minute!*

I rushed outside to the driveway, climbed into the old car, and inserted the cassette into the player.

Nothing—just a buzz. I ejected the tape, turned it end-for-end, and reinserted it.

There was a low hum, then my Uncle Glenn's voice: "So, Hildur, tell me about living in the cabin."

I caught my breath as I heard my mother's voice. "Well, it was a pretty simple place. We didn't have a lot, but then none of our neighbors had any more."

I listened through the whole tape, about thirty-five minutes in total. When it ejected, I stared at the long-lost cassette in my hand and shook my head. "I had it the whole time," I whispered. "Sorry, Glenn, I put you to a lot of trouble."

I didn't learn much from the recording that I didn't already know, but I felt I'd found more than the tape. I had spent countless hours over many years collecting stories about my mother and her family. I had learned more about her than I had hoped to know, more than most children learn about their parents: her mythical upbringing, her spiritual connection to all of nature, her generosity of spirit, her inclusiveness, and her appreciation for life's simple pleasures.

I grew to appreciate how much she had been shaped by her parents, Peter and Lena Back, and how much she valued family. I'd also come to recognize how lucky I was to have had her as a mother, how much I had been shaped by her, and how broad and deep her influence had been on me and our entire family.

I had documented my mother's story. I had captured her memory. I had learned a lot about her and a lot about myself. And now, finally, I had discovered a recording of her voice.

Through the mist of time and the fog of her Alzheimer's, I like to think my mother was saying to me, "I'm so glad you found me. Now, get on with it! Tell my story."

AFTERWORD

It was a little after seven on a brisk spring morning and I was sitting on our porch sipping coffee and admiring the pink-white blossoms and sweet aroma of a crabapple tree that was celebrating the end of winter. A purple finch was perched on a yard light, its rosy head cocked toward the neighbor's birdfeeder.

I was musing about the book I was just finishing, the story of my mother's family. If a blue butterfly had flitted by I would have said it was Mom's spirit stopping by to say hello, almost enough to make me a believer. But no butterfly appeared and I have stayed the heretic that I am. Still, there I was, stimulating my IQ with a big dose of caffeine and soothing my soul with a small dose of nature, as close to a spiritual exercise as I get in my life. Easing into the day is a life-long ritual I picked up from my mother. Maybe she does come to visit me each morning.

And maybe I was with her during much of her journey. I recently heard that when a woman is born she already has all the eggs that she will ever produce. If that's true, then I was there with my mother more than a century ago when she was gestating in my grandmother's womb. I was there when my mother was delivered by a midwife in that little Minnesota north woods log cabin, when she got poked in the eye with a scissors, when she walked through the snow to a one-room school, and when she gazed with excitement at the sun setting over the Montana prairie. My mother's story is our story, her heritage and mine. But it is also an American narrative shared by many.

I had long harbored the desire to document my heritage. When I began my research I was quite methodical: probing my memory for snippets of long ago conversations, tracing the family tree in lines and boxes, itemizing birthdays and the dates of significant events, and searching the web for historical context. With the help of others, I tracked my mother's people back several generations. And, along with millions of others, I also wanted to trace my DNA. I am, according to the tube I spit in, fifty-four percent Scandinavian—no surprise there. I am, however, a little less British and German than I thought and a little more French and Northern European. I am also a little less Neanderthal than I've been accused of.

But I wanted to get to know my ancestors as people; to learn about their struggles and what moved them. I did not find in those drops of spittle, or in those sterile lists of dates and connected boxes on the branches of my family tree, any evidence of great conquerors, or royalty, or high society. There were no famous writers or infamous scoundrels or crooks, no great thinkers or illustrious politicians, and no great world-renowned achievements. I had to accept the fact that my people were common people, people of the land.

Most of us are descendants of common stock and from what I've learned, we're stronger for it. We are all migrants, just with different time frames. Some of us came to this country in chains while others fled poverty or persecution. Like me, many of us can trace our histories to poor immigrants who were looking for a chance at a better life. Whether they came by force or choice, they suffered and sacrificed, worked hard and survived hardships that would devastate many of us. Our country was built on their hard work—they cut the timber, planted the fields, and harvested the crops of a growing nation. When small land holdings were consolidated into large corporate farms, the hard labor necessary to tend the harvest was taken over by new immigrants. Our ancestors' legacy has been our opportunity and our privilege—and our obligation to share what we've gained. Now that I'm firmly entrenched in American society, closing the door to new immigrants, those willing to work hard in pursuit of the same simple dreams as my ancestors, seems to me to be selfish, shallow and shortsighted.

It wasn't until I began interviewing my elders—my mother's surviving sisters and brother—that I began to understand the underlying richness in the lives of these simple folks. How often do any of us deeply listen to our relatives, or anyone else for that matter? We interact over decades with pleasant conversations intended to catch up on current events. And if you're like us Minnesotans, most of the conversations are bunched together in the last few minutes when people are putting on their coats and gloves and are standing by the door waiting for the car to warm up. How often do we set aside the time to focus on one person, face-to-face, and ask, "Tell me about yourself. What's your story?" And all that is rich and valuable is in the asking and the careful listening. Without fail, everyone I wanted to interview agreed without hesitation. They were flattered to be asked and eager to be heard. In each case, we enriched and strengthened our bonds of kinship.

As I listened to my relatives, I began to see more clearly how I—and all of us Back progeny—reflect the family legacy. It is almost primal how so many of us are spiritually tied to the north woods and the out-of-doors. By the good graces of my Stennes cousins, Moose Lake Resort continues as a family retreat, the back-to-our-roots location of periodic family reunions. For several years all of us Taylor kids owned a log cabin together on the shores of a northern lake. My sister Gail and her husband and two of my cousins still own lake-cabin retreats up in the north-country. For years, my sister Sandy lived in a house out in the country where she picked wild berries and baked superb raspberry pie.

When Sue and I were younger, we took our kids camping in the summer, spending weeks roaming back roads and remote campsites. Our children, now grown, do the same with our grandchildren. And every once in a while we all gather together in some out-of-the-way retreat to hike together, eat together, and watch in awe as the sun sets and crimson clouds paint the sky.

While a core of my immediate family—all my brothers and sisters—still cluster in Minneapolis, our children and so many of my nieces and nephews are now distributed nationwide. Scattered as we are, we try to come together every few years for family reunions. And every day I peruse that perturbing Facebook app for their latest doings—my list of "friends" overwhelming dominated by relatives. I am often touched by the loving likes and comments that bounce around among members of my family. I listen in as my children share the events of their lives with their cousins, sustaining connections they made when they were kids gathered together at Moose Lake Resort or sat eager and fidgeting around my mother's Christmas tree.

I am blessed to have a loving family. And now I know how it came about and am thankful for the contributions made by my mother and her parents. I hope that you've found in these stories part of your own heritage, part of your own story. These are real stories about real people and how they lived their lives and how we might better live ours.

ACKNOWLEDGMENTS

Writing this book has been an on-again off-again affair stretching over twenty years. It started when Jennifer Ludeman, the mother of my first grandson, Trace Taylor Ludeman, wanted me to answer a few questions on his behalf about me and my family. She gave me a journal in which she had entered a number of probing questions, each followed by a daunting number of blank pages. Her gift came just as my mother's memory was beginning to fade from Alzheimer's and I realized I needed to urgently attend to documenting her family's history, a project that had hovered at the back of my mind for years but I had been neglecting.

At first, my ambition was simply to document interesting folklore from the oral history we all hear from relatives as we're growing up. But what I managed to pull together from my own memories was disappointingly thin. I quickly shifted to interviewing my mother's aging siblings. I am forever indebted to my Uncle Glenn Back, Aunt Claire Porter and Aunt Ann Stennes—all gone now—for their enthusiastic willingness to put up with my unending questions.

In telling their stories on their behalf, I have tried to sort out truth from fantasy, but like them, I may have added a few details or altered the sequence a bit in order to make the stories lucid. I am, after all, one of them. But the essence of each story is true to their memory. If they were here to read these stories I hope they would nod their heads and smile and say, "Yeah, you got that right." I do know if they were alive today they would see many of their hopes fulfilled. They would recognize the traces of themselves that live in their children, grandchildren and great grandchildren.

After interviewing my aging relatives, it became clear that there was more to their stories than a few disparate vignettes. Increasingly, I was intrigued by how their stories tied together and what greater meaning might lurk in their gestalt. I expanded my research to explore their genealogical roots and the geographical and historical context in which they lived their lives. My Cousin Lynn Lanus's book, *The Hjelm Journey: From Sweden to America*, with her documentation of family genealogy and rich anecdotes, came just at the right time. She accomplished what I would not have had the fortitude to undertake.

In addition to my mother's siblings, I talked to numerous other relatives—my younger brothers Steve, David and Bert, and my older sisters Sandra and Gail. I talked with several of my cousins, nieces and nephews—all of whom were happy to share their recollections and insights. I am especially indebted to my sister, Gail Hanson, and her daughter, Marta, for their foresight and diligence in journaling their interactions with my mother as her memory slipped in and out.

I asked my relatives for help in tracking down old family photographs. I hate to think of the hours they spent searching through the family archives. My special thanks to Marilyn Back and her son, Peter Back; Tom and Cheryl Porter; and my cousins Linnea and Carolyn Forsell.

Among all those old photos was a handsome studio shot of the entire Back family—Peter, Lena and all six children—taken a year or so before Peter Back died. It took a bit of detective work to locate the owner of the photo's copyright. The photo was taken by William H. Scherling who owned the Scherling Photography Studio in Bemidji. He died in 1974 but his granddaughter, Karen Larson, remembered that the studio was purchased by an employee named "Palmer" but didn't know if that was a first or last name. A long-time photographer in Bemidji, Robert Smith of Image Photography, thought that would be Palmer Berg whose son worked at the Bemidji Woolen Mills. It turns out that the fourth generation owner of the 99-year-old store, Bill Batchelder, is a good friend of Palmer Berg and gave me his coordinates. I had delightful conversations with Bill and Palmer who are both history buffs. My thanks to all the kind people who guided my search, and to Palmer Berg for sending me the authorization I needed.

As I poured over the old photos, I was thankful once again to my Aunt Claire Porter for making notes of names and dates on the back of so many. And among those old photos was an unexpected surprise, a school paper written back in 1955 by my Cousin Jim Stennes entitled "My Grandmother: Mrs. Lena Back." I never interviewed my grandmother, but he did, bless his heart. His paper provided some firsthand details that my interviews had not uncovered.

I am also indebted to the Daniels County Museum and Pioneer Town in Scobey, Montana, for giving me the opportunity to have breakfast in an authentic cook car like the one Grandma Back staffed a century ago, and for their amazing collection of pioneer buildings and antique tractors and threshing machines.

My thanks to Deborah Godfrey and Jo Gusic, of TAQA North USA, the oil company that operates the pumpjacks that feed the Hellegaard Battery that sits on the old Hellegaard homestead near Comertown, Montana. The helped me understand the way mineral rights are managed. They also referred me to Marvel Hellegaard who was married to Ole's son, Melvin. For the first years of their marriage, Marvel and Melvin lived on the homestead—in a proper house built next to the old sod cabin. Marvel was a wealth of information and generously shared a copy of the Hellegaard family history.

My wife, Susan, deserves my undying love and appreciation for her encouragement, patience, and understanding over all the years it took me to complete this project. She believed in the worthiness of the effort even when I didn't. She also helped edit the manuscript and helped me interpret the meaning and truth in the stories I was hearing, adding her own insights gained from her long experience as part of my family.

I want to thank Lynne Deur, a writer and poet in her own right, for her encouraging critique and her pointed and constructive editing of an early version of my manuscript. She enthusiastically took on more of a task than she bargained for.

I want to thank my friend and writing coach, James Abraham, for his encouragement. I am especially indebted to Doug Houck, an author of Florida history and my writing instructor, who helped me see how this book could be structured, breaking my long period of writer's block. My thanks also to the members of my writing group for their encouragement, especially Chris (Gary) Chesler for suggesting the concept of the post-WWII car wars.

By their nature, memoir and folklore are prone to fantasy and exaggeration. I admit I composed dialogue of long ago and unrecorded conversations, trying my best to capture the dynamics of what must have occurred given the limits of my memory and the stories I was told. I've come as close to telling the truth as I'm able. I apologize if I got something wrong.

NOTES

1. The geology, history, and future of America's northern forests can be found in publications by the U.S. Forest Service, Northern Research Station. See especially Song, Nianfu, et al, "Forests in the Northern United States," October 19, 2012.

2. More on the Laurentian Plateau, or the Canadian Shield, can be found in numerous sources on the web, including The Editors of the Encyclopedia Britannia, www.britania.com. Good maps of the Plateau can also be found on the web—see Wikipedia and others.

3. There are numerous sources that describe the history of floating logs down the Mississippi to the timber mills above St. Anthony Falls. An interesting account, "A History of Saint Anthony Falls," is provided by the University of Minnesota's National Center for Earth-surface Dynamics: www.esci.umn.edu.

4. Recipe for Swedish Limpa: Mom's recipe for Limpa, a Swedish rye bread made with anise and orange zest, was passed down to her by her mother. An approximation can be made following the Swedish Rye Bread variation of the Dark Pumpernickel Bread recipe in *Betty Crocker's Cookbook*, Ninth edition, IDG Books Worldwide, Inc., An International Data Group Company, 919 E. Hillsdale Boulevard, Suite 400, Foster City, CA 94404, Ninth Edition, 2000, p. 75. Mom's rendition is a bit different.

    1 ½ cups warm water,

    2 pkgs. active dry yeast

¼ cup light molasses

1/3 cup sugar

1 tsp. salt

2 tsp. anise seed

Zest from 1 or 2 oranges

2 tbsp. soft shortening (Mom used Crisco)

2 ½ cups rye flour

2 ½ to 3 cups bleached flour

Instructions: Note Mom's bread making tricks in the Recipe for Yule Kake provided later in these Notes. Knead dough for 5 to 10 minutes or until smooth. Let kneaded dough stand for 15 minutes. Cover and let rise 1 hour until double. Shape into two round loaves, cover and let rise 1 hour on greased cookie sheet. Preheat oven to 375 degrees and bake for 25 to 30 minutes.

5. Lanus, Lynn A., *The Hjelm Journey: From Sweden to America*, self-published, 1999.

6. The North Beltrami Heritage Center, in Kelliher, Minnesota, has a rich collection of artifacts and literature representative of the region. Among their collection are three publications of note: *Kelliher Diamond Jubilee: 75 Years, 1903-1978*; *Down a Long Road: Kelliher Community's 100-Year Journey*; and *On the Trail: A True Romantic Saga from Minnesota's Big Bog*, by Alfred J. Petrowske, 1981.

7. To learn more about the history of Minnesota's Scenic State Park see their website: www.dnr.state.mn.us. Also see the article by Chip Jones, "The Lost 40—A Minnesota Forest Legacy," published on the website www.minnesotafunfacts.com, October 20, 2010. Also see Enger, Leif, "History of Timbering in Minnesota," November 16, 1998: www.news,minnesotapublicradio.org. Enger also gives a chilling account of the Great Hinckley Fire of 1894 that killed 413 people and devastated the towns of Hinckley, Sandstone, Mission Creek, Pokegama, Miller and Askov.

8. Berg, A. Scott, *Lindbergh*, G. P. Putnam's Sons, New York, 1998, p.29.

9. Peter Back's homestead claim: Five years after Peter Back filed his homestead claim his ownership of the property was proofed at

the Land Office at Clear Lake, Minnesota, on October 21, 1914. His claim was defined as: "Lots three and four and the south half of the northeast quarter of Section five in Township one hundred fifty-three north of Range thirty west of the Fifth Principal Meridian, Minnesota, containing one hundred sixty and one-hundredth acres."

One can search Federal Land Patent Records for free via the U.S. National Archives and Research Administration's website or by telephoning their offices: 1-866-272-6272. There are also several private website services that can provide assistance, some charge a fee. You need the name of the claimant and the state where the claim was filed. Claims were defined by Township, Section, and Quarter Section.

All across the vast American landscape, surveyors plotted land into Townships, each six miles on a side. You can see the results best from an airplane, a broad patchwork quilt of squares blanketing the American landscape. An ideal, perfectly square Township (which was rarely true because of variations in terrain and the earth's curvature) was divided into thirty-six, mile-square Sections—much like a checkerboard. Wherever possible, roadways crisscross each township following the section lines. The Sections are numbered from 1 to 36, starting in the north east corner and moving west, numbering 1 through 6 in the first row, then down to the west end of row two, counting eastward from sections 7 through 12, snaking back and forth from row to row. Each Section is 640 acres which is further divided into quarter sections of 160 acres each. An ideal Township contains 144 farms of 160 acres each.

10. The Homestead Act was passed by the Thirty-Seventh Congress and went into effect on May 20, 1862, with several augmentations and variations introduced over subsequent years. The Homestead Act of 1898 opened areas in northern Minnesota to settlement (including Beltrami County and Lower Red Lake where Peter Back filed a claim) and the Act of 1908 opened up areas in northeastern Montana (expanding the size of a claim from 160 to 320 acres and reducing the period to proof from five years to three). Sources: www.americaslibrary.gov, www.nathankramer.com, www.dnr.state.mn.us, www.montanahistory.com, and others.

11. The Treaty of Paris of 1783, negotiated between the United States and Great Britain, ended the revolutionary war, recognized American independence, and established the borders of the new nation. Sources: www.history.state.gov, www.quara.com, www.smithsonianeducation.org, and others.

12. Northwest Angle. Source: Lass, William E., The story behind Minnesota's weirdly shaped northern border, MNOPEDIA, February 4, 2014.

13. How to enjoy lutefisk: Purchase one slab of dried lutefisk (3 to 5 lbs.) and 6 to 8 pieces of dried firewood. Cut lutefisk in three equal lengths with a band saw or a crosscut hand saw. Outside, preferably in a small clearing in the deep woods, build a fire by tenting the firewood inside a circle of melon-sized rocks. When the fire is robust, place the pieces of lutfisk on the fire, meat side down. Invite family or friends to sit around the fire, upwind. Pass around paper cups and a bottle of aquavit. Relax and enjoy. Be sure to fully snuff the fire with a bucket of water before you retire.

14. Recipe for Yule Kake: A good recipe for Yule Kake, a Scandinavian Christmas bread, was in early editions of *Betty Crocker's Cookbook*. Betty Crocker was a fictional homemaker and cook created in 1921 by the predecessor of General Mills, the flour-milling giant located in Minneapolis, in those days the heart of Swedish America. The first Betty Crocker cookbook was published in 1933. My mother's edition, the first with photographs, was published in 1950. My 2000 edition, the Ninth, was published by IDG Books Worldwide, Inc., An International Data Group Company, 919 E. Hillsdale Boulevard, Suite 400, Foster City, CA 94404. The Ninth Edition doesn't include a recipe for yule kake—I don't know where along the line the recipe was dropped. The following recipe was adapted by my mother. It references page 116 of an unknown edition, probably Mom's 1950 issue.

> ¼ cup warm water
>
> 1 pkg. active dry yeast (Mom used 2 pkgs. She mixed the yeast in the warm water in a two cup measuring cup, added a pinch of sugar, and placed the mixture in the oven with the light on—just warm enough on a cold winter day to proof the yeast.)
>
> ¾ cup lukewarm milk (scalded then cooled). (Mom would NOT cool the milk, see below for why.)

½ cup sugar

½ tsp. salt

½ tsp. powdered cardamom (Mom crushed her own, peeling the small dark seeds from the pods and vigorously crushing them between sheets of waxed paper with a rolling pin. A little more than half a teaspoon can't hurt.)

1 egg

2 tbsp. shortening (Mom used Crisco. Trust me on this: don't substitute butter.)

½ cup cut-up citron (Mom used a combination of citron and candied cherries.)

½ cup seedless raisins (Mom plumped the raisins in rum.)

3 ¼ to 3 ½ cups GOLD MEDAL Flour (A loyalist, Mom actually used Gold Medal Flour. Other brands might work, but why risk it?)

Instructions: Here's where Mom went astray of Betty Crocker. In a large bowl, Mom would place all the ingredients in a mixing bowl—minus the yeast—and add half the flour and the still hot milk (to help melt the shortening). She'd mix it well with a wooden spoon and then, with the mixture cooled, she'd stir in the yeast and mix until smooth. She'd then mix in enough, but not all, of the flour for her to handle the still spongy dough. She'd turn the dough out onto a lightly floured counter and knead until smooth—adding handfuls of flour until it felt just right (You're on your own here.) She'd round up the dough in a greased bowl, spreading a bit of Crisco on top with a couple greased fingers, cover the bowl with a dishtowel, and let rise for about 1 ½ hr. (Mom usually put it in her gas oven—the pilot light provided just enough heat. It was the warmest place in the kitchen). She'd punch it down and let it rise for another 45 minutes. She'd shape the dough into two (not one) round loaves on a greased uninsulated baking sheet sprinkled with corn meal. She'd cover the loaves and let rise for another 45 minutes. She'd preheat the oven to 350 degrees, brush the loaves with an egg yolk glaze, and bake for 30 to 40 minutes (usually closer to 40). After they cooled, she'd paint on a little vanilla sugar glaze. Makes two loaves.

Serving suggestion: butter slices of the bread and then toast in a toaster oven until the edges turn a light brown. Serve with coffee and a lump of sugar under your lip.

15. I've given the visiting reverend a fictitious name and origin: Reverend Harold Johnson from Holmes City. According to Ellen Carlson, there were a handful of wandering missionaries who visited homesteaders in the region. One notable Baptist missionary was Reverend G.R. Anderson who originated from Alexandria, Minnesota, five miles from Holmes City. He visited the area regularly and was responsible for founding a number of Swedish Baptist congregations in the area. Source: Carlson, Ellen K., "Battle River—Waskish Baptist Church," *Kelliher Diamond Jubilee, 75 years, 1903-1978*, The North Beltrami Heritage Center, 1978.

16. Recipe for Mush: Mush is a simple porridge made from milk and flour. You heat milk over a medium burner, being careful not to boil, and slowly stir in flour sifted through your fingers until the porridge thickens to the consistency of cooked Cream of Wheat. The aroma of heated milk is like no other. Serve hot with a pat of butter in the center, a drizzle of maple syrup, and a sprinkle of cinnamon. A splash of thick cream adds a rich touch to a humble meal.

17. Train Schedules: Train Schedules were provided through the kindness of Hudson Leighton who drew the information from *The Official Guide of Railways*, February, 1928. Mr. Leighton cautioned that the information could be in error.

18. Source: Leighton, Hudson, citing *The Official Guide of Railways*, February, 1928.

19. "History of Westby, Montana," *Sheridan's Daybreak*, 1970, www.rootsweb.ancestery.com

20. Ibid. "History of Westby, Montana."

21. Ole Hellegaard proved his homestead claim on November 12, 1914, at the land office in Glasgow, Montana. His claim is described as "the southwest quarter of Section ten and the northeast quarter of Section fifteen in Township thirty-seven north of Range fifty-seven east of the Montana Meridian, Montana, containing three hundred twenty acres. The land is still owned by his descendants, now joined with other nearby properties.

22. Barry, John M., *The Great Influenza: The Epic Story of the Deadliest Plague in History*, Viking, the Penguin Group, New York, 2004.

23. Pickett, Mary, "Flu outbreak of 1918-19 claimed 5,000 lives in Montana," *Billings Gazette*, February 5, 2005.
24. Ibid, Barry, *The Great Influenza*.
25. "Spanish "Flu" Vs. German "Flu"", *Plentywood Herald*, Sheridan County, Montana, October 22, 1918.
26. Ibid. "History of Westby, Montana."
27. Sources: World War 1, *The History Channel*, www.history.com; World War One, *Wikipedia*, www.en.m.wikipedia.org
28. In the depression years, many states, including Minnesota, had Old Age Assistance Programs. The programs commonly offered monthly "pension" payments in exchange for a lien on your estate. Source: www.seniorliving.org.
29. There are many versions of the Swedish toe-and-finger-naming games, all spelled differently. I've spelled my mother's version phonetically.

CPSIA information can be obtained
at www.ICGtesting.com
Printed in the USA
FFHW021733180619
53089072-58698FF